APPLYING ARTIFICIAL INTELLIGENCE

APPLYING ARTIFICIAL INTELLIGENCE
THE PRACTITIONER'S HANDBOOK

DAN ROSE JOHANSEN

BIASED
PUBLICATIONS

Published by Biased Publications and distributed by TBK Publishing®.

ISBN 978-87-93116-51-1 (softcover version).

❀ Created with Vellum

Dedicated to Mille

CONTENTS

FOREWORD BY LARS TVEDE

AI is huge - we all know that. However, until you have worked quite a lot with it, you may not know what it's good and bad at. I have personally made thousands of AI prompts and queries, and it works very differently from what I had expected beforehand.

As I see it – now - a Large Language Model (LLM) is like a genius with a huge talent for fantasy and creativity. However, it is mostly not as good at doing arithmetic as the simple calculator that I used in the 1980s. In fact, half the time, it gets basic calculations wrong.

AI tends to get other facts right, but not entirely. For instance, if I ask it about a historical event, it may give a brilliant summary and explanation and describe the year and place it happened, plus the people involved. Fantastic!

Except that two of the people it mentions were not involved, and it happened 16 years later than it stated.

I figured out how to deal with this: Ask several AI models the same questions and compare the results. If they are different, ask each "are you sure that …?"

Sometimes, when working with LMMs, I feel like a police interrogator, if not a psychologist trying to get the truth out of a somewhat unreliable person. Eventually, it tends to work very well.

However, one area where LLMs tend to be brilliant the first time, is when you ask it to come up with product names, brand names, logos, and slogans. This is because generative AI is creative, which is the opposite of what some people who have never used it often believe. And that brings me to the point that you can use AI to automate tasks and thus save a ton of money and speed up stuff. For instance, in figuring out how proteins fold in 3D, or tagging, illustrating, and summarising huge amounts of text in a jiffy. But you can also use for hyper-creative tasks, such as composing music, creating poems and being visually artistic. These are very different tasks.

So, there is stuff to do, but just comprehending the options is a challenge. For instance, as I began writing this foreword, there were 484,932 AI models uploaded to the Hugging Face website. Each of these was trained for a specific task, and the number is doubling approximately every 3.4 months. This corresponds to 11.5 times more per year.

Get out the calculator!

This sounds like there will be approx. 5.3 million different AI models at the end of 2024.

Incidentally, if we roll the rule forward to early 2030, we will have well over 1 trillion different AI models by then, hooray. But, wait-a-minute. That sounds crazy, so, perhaps not. But on the other hand, perhaps yes, I'll get to that. But in general, I believe that there are three applications of AI that will be particularly interesting:

1. AI at scale is the use of AI to solve large problems that require the processing of massive amounts of data. This is an area of AI that is growing rapidly, and it has the potential to revolutionize a wide range of industries, from healthcare to finance. AI at scale could be used to analyse large amounts of medical data to develop new treatments for diseases. It could also be used to improve the efficiency of supply chains and manufacturing processes, for instance.
2. AI orchestration is the combined use of multiple AI models. This is important because AI models can often be better at solving problems if they work together. AI orchestration could be used to coordinate the work of multiple AI models to detect and prevent fraud in financial transactions. It could also be used to improve the accuracy of weather forecasts.
3. Personal AI is the use of AI to deliver personalized services to individuals. This has the potential to have a major impact on our lives. Personal AI can be used to give us tailored recommendations for products, services, and experiences. It can also be used to help us manage our health and finances. Personal AI could be used to give us personalized recommendations for movies, music, and books. It could also be used to help us learn new languages and skills, to be our education coach (à la Khan's Academy), our fitness instructor, food mentor, etc.

I believe that all three of these AI areas have the potential to be transformative. AI at scale has the potential to solve some of the world's most pressing problems. AI orchestration has the potential to make AI more powerful and efficient. And personal AI has the potential to make our lives easier and more enjoyable.

Now, going back to the previously mentioned ridiculous sounding 1 trillion different AI models by 2030. This number is not my forecast, but I don't think it is impossible either. If most people by then have a personal AI trained on them as individuals, and if each of these personal AI models is in fact not really one model but based on AI orchestration with a heterogeneous symphony of models working in concert on helping each individual, then yes, we might get there, or close to it. I mean – we might get close to the trillion AI models in 2030, or something thereabouts.

A factor in the growth of Ai is that it is becoming exponentially cheaper. Partly due to ever-better dedicated chip types, we have been able to drive down the costs of training AI models with a psychedelic half-life that is sometimes 5-6 weeks. In fact, there is an expectation that the training of an AI model that cost over $4 million in 2020 will be reduced to just between $30 and $300 in 2030. By which time, it should be said, AI may also have passed a Touring Test and thus be as least as smart as a typical human for all tasks. Two years after that, it will probably be smarter on all tasks than the smartest human that ever lived.

The field of AI has long been shrouded in technical jargon and algorithmic complexity, often alienating those it aims to benefit. Johansen's work diverges from this path, emphasising that the application of AI is fundamentally different from traditional IT. Where traditional IT focuses on systems, infrastructure and code, AI is an explorative journey into the realms of human behaviour, decision-making, and business processes. This differentiation is critical; it shifts our perspective from viewing AI as a mere tool to understanding it as a transformative agent in business and society.

The Todai Method, as meticulously detailed in this handbook, is built upon this very premise. In a world where AI is rapidly evolving, the Todai Method acts as a compass, guiding practitioners towards a user-centric and discovery-driven approach. This is especially pivotal as we stand on the brink of a generative AI revolution, where the ability of AI to create, predict, and decide will significantly influence every aspect of our lives.

Johansen makes a compelling case for an approach which ensures that AI solutions are not just technically sound but are also aligned with the real-world needs of businesses and their customers. In doing so, it bridges the gap between the theoretical potential of AI and its practical, value-driven application in the business world. And as we venture deeper into the era of generative AI, where machines can create content, the importance of a human-centric approach becomes more pronounced.

In conclusion, "Applying AI - The Practitioner's Handbook" is a timely and invaluable resource for anyone looking to harness the power of AI in their business.

I hope you will enjoy reading it as much as I did!

Lars Tvede

P.S. Hey GPT: "When Lars finished writing this foreword, Hugging Face had 485,008 models. How long did it take Lars to write the foreword?"

INTRODUCTION

I've been working with artificial intelligence for almost ten years and am impressed by what the technology can do.

Recent breakthroughs like OpenAI's ChatGPT and Stable Diffusion from Stability have garnered global attention and showcased remarkable results. However, confusion around the words "artificial" and "intelligence" mystify and obscure their practical use. From a distance, AI appears to combine information technology tools to develop systems capable of producing predictions, estimates, forecasts, projections, and other types of assessments that come with a probability. Let's stay with the statement that AI is a label for IT tools that make predictions.

It can be extremely difficult to determine which problems will benefit from AI and how these projects can be steered to successful completion (or abandoned before they run amok). Between 75% and 80% of AI projects fail because inadequate tools are applied to problems, or the projects are mismanaged.

This book is for anyone involved with identifying processes or areas where AI can improve performance. It will help you to build business cases that justify your efforts (or lead to an early and inexpensive rejection) and help you to organise projects for its implementation. Anyone involved with improving organisational performance can benefit. Rookie or pro. Entrepreneur or civil servant. Architect or engineer. Executive or operational agent. Anyone.

The secret behind any successful IT project is sharing a standard method, understanding its vocabulary and the steps involved, and early user engagement. The method described is *specifically* designed for AI projects, and it works best when the entire team follows its recommendations.

Applying the following principles can bring your AI project's success rate far beyond 90%. This requires abandoning hopeless projects early, completing projects with a promising business case fast, and getting users to embrace the outcome produced by the systems.

As well as learning about AI, its fundamental components, and its practical aspects, you'll discover how to:

- Spot areas in your organisation where AI can provide value.
- Develop a systematic approach to applying and developing new AI solutions. This includes creating a business case, managing projects effectively, and ensuring user adoption.
- Effectively collect data for your AI solutions.
- Build AI that users love and are eager to adopt.

Adopting new technology too early can be expensive and require significant investment to achieve marginal value functionality. On the other hand, if you adopt it too late, you risk missing out on potential savings, better customer service, and other benefits that could improve your operation and competitive position. However, the pace of AI development is accelerating rapidly. Off-the-shelf solutions can solve mundane problems at very reasonable cost points. In fact, the cost of using AI is dropping at an astonishing rate.

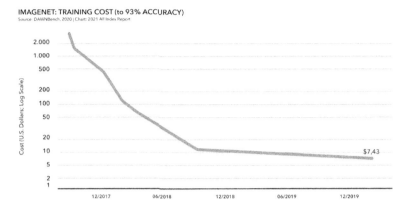

Figure 1: The cost of training an AI-model to 93% accuracy

The graph above shows that in 2017, it cost over $2,000 in computer power to train a model to 93% accuracy. In 2020, the same model cost as little as $7.43 – a 300-fold cost reduction in three years. Training time also dramatically improved. Thirteen days in 2017 dropped to as few as 2 minutes and 38 seconds in 2020. In 2023, the time and costs are so low that measuring them no longer makes sense.

AI is becoming more affordable, and its performance is significantly improving. For example, ImageNet's image recognition accuracy improved from 83% in 2013 to over 99% in 2021.

The graph might indicate that progress has slowed, but a one percentage point improvement from 98 to 99 corresponds to a 50% reduction in the error rate. Such a reduction can be a game-changer for a business case, turning a no-go into a no-brainer.

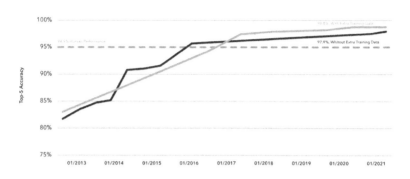

Figure 2: ImageNet challenge: top-5 accuracy

People make approximately 6% errors when assessing an image. This means that in 2016 AI assessments surpassed those of humans. Since 2021, AI has become exceptionally proficient, and it can now outperform people – even experts – in more and more areas.

Investment in AI is rapidly growing and showing an almost exponential increase. In 2015, global investment was around $13 billion. By 2021, the figure had surged to almost $100 billion.

Although AI is part of *information technology* (IT), your implementation will fail if you attempt to prepare and run an AI project like a traditional IT one. AI requires everyone within and around the project to understand what AI is, how it works, what outcomes it can produce, and how those outcomes can be translated into operational value. My method breaks down an AI project into a step-by-step approach. This includes the:

1. inspiration phase, where you can identify what AI can do for your business
2. discovery phase, where you set your objectives and design your solution
3. data phase and the challenges associated with inaccurate or low-quality data, as well as data-related ethical and legal issues
4. development phase, where you build your solution

5. implementation phase, where you deploy your AI-driven solution into a human context
6. monitoring phase, where you make sure that the solution works and produces value

Remember that the reason to adopt AI is that it provides specific business advantages. For example, it could save you time or improve product quality. As AI evolves and matures, it will bring countless new opportunities. And there's no need to wait – there are already countless practical ways to use it.

I have written this book to help you do just that.

CHAPTER 1
MAKING BOOK-KEEPING MORE PRODUCTIVE

In 2013, I joined a startup called Billy, which developed user-friendly accounting software for small businesses and independent contractors. While the software simplified accounting, users had to input invoice data, a tedious and time-consuming process manually. This sparked the idea for a new startup, Paperflow, to provide an inexpensive and easy-to-use service that could automatically read and interpret payable invoices and enter the data into the accounting software.

Existing solutions were geared towards big companies and needed a customised set up for each creditor. This made them too expensive and complex for small businesses. People spent countless hours reading and entering invoice data, causing unnecessary costs and errors in financial reports. We aimed to make the process more affordable and productive by offering a simple solution that didn't require custom implementation. In other words, we wanted to offer small business owners a book-keeping solution that worked at the click of a button.

We believed there was a vast global market for such a service and were confident we could develop an easy-to-use solution. Small business owners could say goodbye to tedious manual accounting operations and devote more time to growing their businesses.

How could this not become an instant success?

CHAOTIC FIRST YEAR

We started with a small team of three: the Billy founder, a chief technology officer (CTO), and me as marketing manager. I prepared for our launch while the CTO was coding. The CTO jumped ship five months later, and I took over development and product management. That meant I had to find developers and figure out how to proceed.

First, we tried the traditional if-then-what-else approach. That failed, so we introduced AI tools. At that time, we were testing an open-source coding library called Tesseract, an off-the-shelf software that used optical character recognition (OCR). It was the go-to library for reading alphanumeric text on images and had been around for over twenty years. In theory, the software should have been able to read documents out of the box. We only needed to input images and to get the results: words, numbers, and their positions in the document.

Or so we thought. Tesseract was an AI or machine learning-based system, and we didn't fully comprehend what that meant. I'm not sure that the words "machine learning" or "artificial intelligence" were ever spoken in the office.

As we studied the results, we realised we were working with something different from traditional IT. We couldn't say if the OCR was correct when we scanned a new invoice. Parsing values such as amounts and dates from invoices was challenging if we couldn't be sure the letters and numbers the OCR read were correct.

It dawned on us that the OCR's accuracy was contingent on the fonts and layouts used, and we'd been unaware of the volume of invoice variations prospective clients would bring. We had limited knowledge of the performance we could expect from our solution before we saw it work in production.

OCR technology has existed since the mid-1960s and was more affordable, with lower prices and more options available by 2015. While working on Paperflow, Google launched a high-quality cloud-based API for OCR that could be completed at a much lower cost. We decided to use that to deliver the values, allowing us to focus on identifying relevant content in the invoices. However, interpreting text and numbers was difficult, especially when identifying the data elements necessary to determine the creditor's identity, invoice and due date, quantity, product description, unit price, discount, order number, total amount, VAT, and other relevant information. This task is known as *entity recognition* (NER) in AI terminology. While the term existed in academic circles, it wasn't widely recognised or applied in the industry or available in off-the-shelf AI tools.

We were dependent on immature technology. While the algorithms now referred to as AI had been around since the 1960s in academia, they were rarely applied in an operational context. Most of the material on the subject was either promotional fluff from software vendors or highly technical papers from academia.

As we approached the end of the first year, we needed to speed up product development, and we hired our first developer with AI experience. He started working on the problem and testing different machine-learning approaches. We were finally making progress.

FIRST AND CONFUSING FEEDBACK

Next to the data recognition engine, we also needed a user-facing application enabling book- keepers to approve the results. This would submit invoices by email to the AI engine, which presented the results on the interface within 30-60 seconds. The user could approve or correct the data, transferring and committing it to the accounting software.

After six months of hard work, we finally had a web application to present to potential customers. This was a significant milestone, as the product was now becoming tangible. Such solutions weren't readily available or a standard feature in any accounting software, and our potential users were unfamiliar with their potential. We were excited to showcase something new that could substantially improve productivity.

However, although people were curious, they had numerous objections.

We were trying to develop a seamless "one-click" invoice workflow that was inexpensive, easy to use, and timesaving. But bookkeepers weren't looking for an easier way of doing things. They didn't want the flow to be automated and hands-free. Some said that manually entering invoices "gave them a feel for the state of the businesses," and others said that unless the results were 100% correct, it was useless.

We were surprised that the possibility of saving time and avoiding typing mistakes wasn't met with more enthusiasm. Also, the book-keepers wanted our solution embedded in their accounting software before considering using it. Some recognised our solution's improved efficiency in processing invoices but didn't want to bother with an additional application. We had to find a way forward.

Our assumption that extracting invoice data was challenging and that bookkeepers would independently determine the optimal way to use it was wrong. They wanted access to the functionality within their existing software, making things much more complicated.

It didn't help that the book-keepers had differing opinions about interpreting identical invoices. While one identified a specific field as a "project number," another considered it an "invoice number," and a third labelled it an "order number."

We also had problems making the AI engine produce high-quality output fast enough, lacking the required expertise. Our hiring approach had been to recruit anyone with machine-learning experience. However, AI is a vast field with numerous specialisations, and our team's AI skills weren't an ideal fit for the product we were developing.

As a temporary solution, we opted to avoid AI for a while. Instead, we developed a simple rule-based approach. Surprisingly, we discovered that such rules could yield an accuracy rate of up to 60%. Although not competitive, it was a starting point.

Our product could now extract data from invoices, but the accompanying web application still didn't align with the users' requirements. A stand-alone solution meant we had to construct and maintain all the integrations for differing accounting software systems — a demanding job for our small team.

We decided to streamline our product scope. That entailed eliminating the web application, making us solely an API-based platform. That way, we could concentrate on a specific aspect of the book- keeping process: identifying data on payable invoices. And it distinguished us from our competitors, who all relied on web or desktop applications.

BETA-LAUNCH

We believed that we now had a *minimal viable product*. The accuracy of invoice parsing was insufficient to revolutionise accounting, but it was enough to launch a functional product and generate revenue. We could have invested more time crafting a superior solution, but we needed to prove we could generate revenue to keep the funding coming in.

We worked with Paperflow's co-founder Billy (which had more than 10,000 users at that time) to kick off the beta launch. But one thing is to convince a SaaS vendor to include our service in their offering, and another is to win over users and make them happy.

For Billy to use Paperflow's invoice reader, they had to integrate with our API. Invoices were sent to our service automatically, the information parsed and then returned. They had no problem implementing the API in a technical sense, but dealing with the uncertainty of AI was new to them. When Billy sent us an invoice and received the results, they didn't know if they could trust them. The results could be perfect with all the invoice data read correctly by our software, or it could be wrong. Most cases would be correct and few incorrect. That would never happen in traditional IT, but explaining the difference was tricky. The room for interpretation of results also made testing harder. Implementing AI with this first customer was supposed to be an easy and sure thing but dragged on and took a toll on the team.

HUMANS IN THE LOOPS – WHAT WE DID RIGHT

Following the release of our initial platform version, I attended a machine learning Meetup in Copenhagen hosted by Tradeshift (a Danish startup that primarily dealt with electronic invoices) where they presented their solution for reading invoices from images or PDFs. Tradeshift was working on the same problem, and their presentation gave me valuable insight.

Tradeshift's approach involved collecting data by analysing previously entered invoices and using a program to identify the position of values on the invoices. This required less effort and achieved more data than Paperflow's manual marking of each word. The downside was lower data quality.

The reason is as follows: The book-keeper entered "100" as the total amount. The program then searched for "100" and marked it as the total amount. This position was used as training data to teach a machine-learning model to read other invoices. The benefit of this approach was that you can process many invoices at minimal expense and quickly obtain a significant amount of training data. However, the program's identification of "100" as the total amount might be inaccurate, as "100" could also appear elsewhere on the invoice. Additionally, users make more errors when entering data without AI forming part of the training data.

Tradeshift had achieved an 82% accuracy rate, on par with the market benchmark at that time. However, the poor data quality used to train the models curtailed improvement. At Paperflow, we wanted to surpass this accuracy rate. One solution was to obtain more high-quality training data, but doing that as a startup with limited funds was problematic.

We decided to offer a premium product version with a human verifying the AI output before passing the data to the customer's system. The verification step would allow us to gather high-quality data and get the AI accuracy past the 82% standard while having the customer cover the costs.

Our mistake was in announcing this version would yield 100% accuracy. Even a four-eye principle doesn't give absolute accuracy. Eliminating errors required other processes and controls and would be extremely expensive. Even if we had no errors, the book-keepers would still disagree about correct values. Our 100% claim led to negative feedback from users who found errors. We changed the claim to "equal to the average bookkeeper."

This also failed.

Like anyone, book-keepers tend to believe they perform better than average. Although we stumbled with our marketing messages, the human-in-the-loop product development approach succeeded. We found customers who recognised the benefits and were willing to pay a premium. The feature allowed us to gather significant amounts of high-quality data, which our competitors lacked. Data quality became our strategic advantage.

At Paperflow's inception, we'd assumed that acquiring "some training data" would be a onetime task that could be completed within a few weeks or months. In fact, data acquisition became a continuous operation that at one point involved almost fifty full-time employees—a vast difference from our initial expectations.

GROWTH

New and improved data meant our product's accuracy increased, leading to an increase in our client base. But we still suffered from having launched prematurely. The system was complex to maintain and keep online, consuming valuable time and resources we could have used for product improvement. As a result, we were slow in introducing new features and accommodating customised requests. Despite this, we managed to sustain our growth.

After limiting the product to an API-based engine, our go-to-market approach shifted. We now had to convince accounting system providers (such as local providers like Billy and Uniconta and international providers like Microsoft Business Central) to incorporate our service into their offerings. That caused us to lose direct contact with end users. We also lost control of how the predicted values were presented in the different accounting software solutions.

For example, our solution predicted the document type, such as an invoice or credit note. Regardless of the document type, we'd still be able to predict most of the values found. However, the prediction appeared empty if the AI couldn't find a value. Sometimes, the payment date wasn't on the invoice, or the AI couldn't find it – even when it did find the payment date, the accounting software might not present it to the user. This was frustrating as it was hard for the user to identify whether Paperflow, the accounting software, or the invoice was the problem.

Relinquishing control over how the results were presented to users was more significant than we'd anticipated. To prevent users from having a negative experience, we had to refine the onboarding process for accounting software providers. Convincing them to disclose how they applied Paperflow's product wasn't easy. This challenge is now recognised for AI solutions as they tend to be in the backend, but it took us by surprise at the time.

RESEARCH AND DEVELOPMENT DON'T ALWAYS PAY OFF

We aimed to create and provide the most accurate invoice scanner possible at an affordable price. By accumulating more and better data, our service quality continued to improve. We then took a more research and development-focused approach to enhance the AI algorithms and collaborated with the University of Copenhagen. Our goal was to outperform our competitors by being at the forefront of technology.

We focused on probabilistic programming, a branch of AI modelling that wasn't widely used in an operational environment at the time – it had only recently started gaining momentum. Even in academia, it wasn't a significant field, although the basis for probabilistic models has been around for a few hundred years. We invested significant effort in it as a potential avenue for improving accuracy, but despite its initial promise, it didn't yield significant results. The technology was still too immature, and the resulting service was unstable and prone to crashes, requiring even more time and resources for main-tenance.

In retrospect, we should have directed this effort towards improving the core product and enhancing user satisfaction.

GOING GLOBAL

We envisioned Paperflow to be easily scalable internationally. Once we had a functional solution and had gained traction in our local market, we decided to invest in expanding abroad. Again, our efforts didn't succeed like we'd hoped for. With Danish companies receiving more than 20% of their invoices from abroad, we were confident about having ample training data. However, we'd wrongly assumed that our AI could read invoices from other countries effectively. Moreover, believing that European countries less digitally advanced than Denmark would find AI-powered invoice reading appealing was also wrong. While extracting data from a document and inputting it into an accounting software system appears identical worldwide, the willing-ness to automate it varies significantly.

Our go-to-market approach also posed a challenge to international expansion. We had to identify accounting software providers, convince them to cooperate, get them onboard and integrate Paperflow into their offerings. However, cloud-based services like Paperflow weren't widely accepted in many countries. Furthermore, we lacked a position and network abroad that would enable us to reach potential partners.

For those we attempted to get on board, we met an even broader range of accounting workflows, which made it complicated.

The prevalence of paper-based business documents in many countries posed another challenge. Even in countries such as Sweden and the UK, geographically close to Denmark, around 50% of invoices were still paper-based and delivered by mail. This starkly contrasted with Denmark, where less than 10% of invoices were paper-based, and 90% were emailed as PDFs. As a result, the task for our AI was more complex, as it had to read a more significant number of physically printed invoices that varied in appearance.

HAPPY ENDING

Paperflow ended up in a good place. It didn't become the unicorn all entrepreneurs dream of, but it did well despite the many challenges. In August 2022, a large SAP provider acquired it, and its revenue continues to grow.

The main things we learned from the Paperflow experience were:

- Despite proof of value, users are generally reluctant to embrace new technology, which hinders technical progress. Implementing innovations requires identifying the technology enthusiasts and visionaries prepared to work with seemingly premature solutions and iron out inconveniences.
- Scaling innovative solutions requires substantial user involvement, education and coaching.
- It is hard to predict how users will respond to output that is not 100% accurate. The book-keepers with whom we communicated expected absolute accuracy. They overestimated or ignored their own accuracy rate and demanded much more from an automated system.
- Users aren't necessarily motivated by improvements in productivity. If such improvements seem to reduce their level of control, they resist the change.

- Sticking with tried and tested AI technology will likely give faster and less expensive results. Trying to get ahead while at the forefront of technology is risky. There are ample opportunities for improvements elsewhere in most projects.
- Data quality plays a significant role in the outcome of any AI-based system. The cost of generating enough quality data can become the most significant issue.
- Because it's hard to foresee what it will take to produce a certain level of AI accuracy, users must be involved early in the project to validate accuracy needs. If they eventually reject the output accuracy, the project will fail. Even when performance improves, a bad reputation can be hard to rectify.
- Certain problems can only be addressed using AI-based systems. Identifying these problems and understanding the process of preparing a business case and what it takes to run a project requires that all stakeholders have a foundational understanding of AI technology. This makes AI projects different from other IT projects where the stakeholders don't need a common foundational understanding of the technologies.
- Using an AI-specific project management method, including a shared vocabulary, improves any aspect of a project compared to a trial-and-error happy-go-lucky approach.

Building an AI-based company from scratch paid for my AI education, taught me how to apply it, and showed me all the pitfalls. I'd like to pass on that experience to you.

CHAPTER 2
DEFINING AND DEMYSTIFYING AI

Artificial intelligence is information technology that relies on algorithms known as *machine learning* that use examples or observations (data) to perform a given task. The fundamental difference between artificial intelligence and other types of information technology, such as deterministic algorithms (classical IT), is that the quality of output from an AI-driven system relies on data and instructions instead of instructions alone.

When data is specified as examples and observations, this excludes systems that use instructions and data such as databases or user input. The word "data" can include a subtext that there's a single true or correct answer. Conversely, the words "observation" and "example" suggest perception is part of the equation and there might be more than one version of the "truth." Examples or observations are based on what happened, implying that not every possibility is covered. For example, *examples of shopper behaviour* are less convincing than *data of shopper behaviour*.

These subtexts and implications colour everything in AI and explain why this technology can be very different from other IT areas. In this book, "data" means examples and observations.

Some people define artificial intelligence as machines able to perform tasks typically associated with humans or machines that can learn and perceive information in ways like humans. This definition is flawed. The reason for this may be due to the name *artificial intelligence*.

MACHINE LEARNING

Although the terms *artificial intelligence* and *machine learning* are used interchangeably in this book, they have slightly different meanings.

Machine learning is a subset of artificial intelligence that performs better (regarding results) when provided with data. According to Tom Mitchell, a renowned computer scientist:

A computer program is said to learn from experience E with respect to some class of tasks T and performance measure P if its performance at tasks in T, as measured by P, improves with experience E. [1]

Algorithms or systems that enhance their performance with more data (examples) are considered to be able to learn. Most AI systems currently in operational use are based on machine learning, and his book's recommendations are exclusively related to AI based on machine learning. That also covers all AI encountered in a business setting.

ARTIFICIAL INTELLIGENCE – A MISLEADING NAME

Artificial intelligence is a misleading name for a set of information technology tools that rely on data as opposed to those that only need instructions. It's primarily the term *intelligence* that's problematic.

Human intelligence involves much more than just the pattern recognition that AI uses. There isn't a single accepted definition of what human intelligence is. However, our ability to process information, make intuitive decisions, or come to conclusions is invaluable. So is our ability to learn from others and from experience. Designing computer systems to do the same seems like a good idea. If we label our abilities to learn and process information as "intelligence", it makes sense to label computer systems that resemble those human capabilities as "artificial". Based on this logic, the term *artificial intelligence* was coined in the mid-1950s as an academic discipline to describe how machines could act and perform like human beings – or at least act and behave like *rational* human beings, including the ability to learn and improve continuously.

This might still be the objective in academia, but your ambition is precisely the opposite in an operational context. You want to take the human *out* of the equation – especially elements based on ignorance, intuition, prejudice, feelings and bias.

You want tools that make reliable predictions on which you can base operational decisions and activities. You also want these systems to improve their performance over time, generating increased value in their wake.

Example-based computing is a better name for AI, but it's too late to change. And "artificial intelligence" has a cooler vibe. We must deal with any confusion about what this means when encountering it.

IT tools that can make increasingly reliable predictions using algorithms that rely on data are called "artificial intelligence." That's all you need to remember.

DEFINING AI IS ESSENTIAL

The term artificial intelligence is misleading, and the hype surrounding it in the public sphere causes people to have different perceptions of what it is and does. They could carry these disparate perceptions into your operational environment, leading to confusion and concern.

An unclear definition also makes communication and expectation management challenging. One person could believe AI comprises sentient thinking machines. Another might think it's a utopian concept, and a third that it just means algorithms based on instructions. These people won't see the same risks and opportunities as each other and will have difficulty cooperating.

The most straightforward definition to use is "tools and techniques that combine algorithms and examples or observations which can make predictions."

CAT OR DOG?

An excellent example to explain basic AI concepts and vocabulary is a system that can decide if a picture shows a cat or a dog.

Such a system will consist of algorithms. An *algorithm* is a sequence of instructions similar to a recipe. Following a recipe is the same as using an algorithm, and creating a new recipe is equivalent to designing a new algorithm. Some algorithms are complex and mathematically intensive like gourmet recipes.

Algorithms are sets of instructions that use data to make predictions. The output generated by the AI image recognition algorithm is known as a *model* – a mathematical representation of the information provided to the algorithm. The process of achieving this representation is referred to as *learning*. The process in which AI algorithms use the given examples to build the model is known as *training*. Applying the model to a new data set generates a new *prediction*. Sorting pictures of cats and dogs requires AI image recognition (or computer vision) to identify and interpret objects, features, and details in the images.

The process typically involves training an AI model on a large dataset of images. The dataset's images are labelled with each image associated with a specific category or class. The AI model learns to recognise patterns and features in the images that correlate with these classes.

Once trained, the model can analyse new, unlabelled images and predict their class based on what it's learned. In this case, the model can identify whether a new picture is of a cat or a dog. Such AI image recognition systems are available off the shelf and can be used directly on operational data.

The number of example images required to train the algorithm varies depending on several factors, which can't be predetermined. The more the animals look alike and the more variances in their backgrounds, the more examples are necessary. A more controlled environment, such as a consistent white background, requires fewer examples. Furthermore, the number needed depends on the desired accuracy of the model's predictions. Increasing the amount of relevant data enhances its accuracy. For example, if the job entails identifying different breeds of dogs, 500 images of different species are more valuable than 1,000 images of a single breed.

The unpredictability of AI means we can't foresee what input X will produce as output Y until the solution is developed. This unpredictability makes the preparation of business cases for AI projects much more complicated than for traditional IT projects.

DATA, INFORMATION AND PREDICTIONS

In academia, data and information are considered synonymous. However, in a business context, they have distinct meanings.

Data refers to unstructured sets of values that aren't particularly useful on their own. Data can be compiled, interpreted, or combined to create information that can be used for decision-making.

When AI solutions make predictions, such as determining whether an image contains a cat or a dog, they transform data (the image) into *information* (the prediction). Therefore, AI systems can be viewed as solutions that convert data into information that can be employed in operational decision-making processes.

RELATIONS AND CASUALTIES

AI models can make very reliable predictions. Ask ChatGPT a question, and you may be surprised by the level of detail it returns. Such predictions may lead some to assume that AI models have a causal understanding of the world.

That isn't the case.

AI algorithms operate on statistical patterns. They cannot grasp the underlying mechanisms that generate those patterns in the first place.

For example, an AI model intended to predict if a person will purchase a product may recognise that individuals in specific age ranges or income brackets are likelier to buy it. However, the model can't explain why this is the case or whether there's a causal link between these factors and purchasing behaviour.

We must analyse the underlying mechanisms that link variables to identify causal relationships. This involves examining the factors that cause a specific outcome and determining how altering those factors can impact the outcome. AI algorithms aren't intended for this type of causal analysis.

The limitations of AI causality can have profound implications regarding decision making. Without a causal understanding of the world, AI models may produce wildly inaccurate predictions when the underlying mechanisms change. For example, suppose a model predicts that individuals in a certain age group are more likely to default on a loan than those in another age group. On the surface, denying loans to those individuals would make sense. However, their default risk could be low due to other causal factors that the model doesn't consider. For example, perhaps age is just a proxy of how well-attached a person is in the job market. If so, people with a short education and longer job history would be treated unfairly.

Because AI models don't have a causal understanding of the world, they might be unable to generalise well to new situations. If the statistical patterns the model learned from the training data don't indicate any underlying causal mechanisms, the model's predictions could be unreliable when faced with new data.

THREE (OR SO) WAYS FOR AI TO LEARN FROM DATA

Each of the three ways for AI algorithms to use data to build models suited for a particular situation has its own advantages and disadvantages. Sometimes, a combination of approaches is the best answer, but you don't need to comprehend their technical intricacies. If you understand their general principles, you can apply them appropriately.

Supervised learning is when an algorithm is trained using historical data that contains only correct answers. The training data includes examples of inputs along with their corresponding outputs. For example, historical sales records containing actual prices can be used if the goal is to predict housing prices. These records also contain data points such as the property's age, area, and postcode, which the model can use to predict prices. Actual sales prices guide the algorithm, enabling it to learn from the past and make accurate predictions. The primary objective of a supervised learning algorithm is to develop models that can accurately predict these outputs for new input data.

Sometimes, the data might not have the necessary labels (answers) we need. In such cases, we must add those labels, called labelling or annotation manually. For example, for AI to recognise pictures of cats and dogs, we must label each picture as a cat or a dog.

Label	Features			
Price	Postcode	Number of rooms	m2	Year built
€250k	2000	3	190	1990
€140k	2200	4	140	1960
€350k	2900	3	230	1930

Table 1: Labelling

Supervised learning is the most applied form of AI in operational use today. It's relatively easy to tell the algorithm what you want it to accomplish. This makes it simple for AI designers to understand when compared with other types of AI. The downside of supervised learning is that it requires labelled data, which is typically of poor quality or costly to obtain or improve.

Unsupervised learning doesn't require labelled data during training. For example, consider the housing price data mentioned earlier, but this time without the corresponding prices.

Features			
Postcode	Number of rooms	m2	Year built
2000	yellow	190	1990
2200	red	140	1960
2900	White	230	1930

Table 2: Features

One common application is clustering, where data is grouped into similar entities based on their characteristics. For example, this could involve grouping houses with similar features that would interest a potential buyer who's shown interest in another home.

The same approach can also provide song recommendations like those a user has recently listened to, even without them expressly indicating a preference. The advantage of unsupervised learning is that it doesn't require costly data labelling, although its practical applications may be limited in many operational situations. However, there are more use cases for unsupervised learning, and it's likely to become more prevalent, especially when combined with supervised learning.

Reinforcement learning involves training an algorithm to solve problems through a trial-and-error approach. The algorithm randomly attempts strategies and receives feedback through rewards or penalties based on performance. The algorithm adjusts its approach through repeated iterations and gradually improves its ability to make reliable predictions.

Reinforcement learning is the least frequently used type of machine learning in an operational context. However, it's gaining increasing attention, particularly after the achievements of companies such as DeepMind, which used reinforcement learning (among other techniques) to teach its AI to play the board game Go and ultimately beat the world champion.

A critical challenge for reinforcement learning algorithms is a safe and affordable training environment. Imagine attempting to train an AI for a self-driving car using reinforcement learning. Whenever the car crashes, hits an obstacle or violates traffic laws, the algorithm makes a minor adjustment to its model. This process must be repeated millions of times until the car can safely navigate roads and comply with traffic regulations. Such a trial-and-error approach is unsustainable when considering time, cost, and safety constraints.

A solution to the challenge of creating safe and affordable training environments is to build virtual worlds and environments where the algorithms can train. Companies like NVIDIA and Unity are investing in products that enable the creation of such in-silicon environments, commonly called "digital twins." Training algorithms in these digital twins can significantly reduce the cost and time required to train models.

The challenge lies in accurately representing the natural world in the digital twin. If the digital twin isn't an accurate representation, the trained model may not perform well in the real world. On the other hand, if we could perfectly represent the world digitally, it would eliminate the need for AI to solve many problems. For example, we can use AI to predict how long it would take to drive from A to B at a given time of day. With a perfect digital twin, we could simulate and know the exact time. We'd no longer need to rely on probability.

Newer forms of learning can be considered hybrid models rather than entirely distinct categories.

Self-supervised learning combines elements of both supervised and unsupervised learning. An algorithm can take unlabelled data and automatically use it to generate labelled data, which can be used for supervised learning tasks. That's a huge benefit since labelling costs are reduced while you still get the prediction ability from supervised learning.

Self-supervised learning generates training data because parts of a training set are removed or changed, such as predicting a missing word from a sentence, reconstructing a corrupted image, or predicting the next frame in a video. The model is then trained to predict the missing or corrupted part of the input and uses these predicted labels to learn a representation of the data that captures its underlying structure.

An example of this training data could be: "Why did the __ cross the road?" With enough texts and randomly removed words, an algorithm will learn that chickens often cross the road. This is how most *large language models* (LLMs) are trained.

Semi-supervised learning combines supervised and unsupervised learning approaches. It involves using two datasets: a labelled dataset with known outputs and an unlabelled dataset with unknown outputs. Typically, the labelled dataset is smaller than the unlabelled dataset.

The semi-supervised learning approach starts by training a model using the labelled dataset. This model predicts the outputs for the unlabelled dataset, which effectively labels the unlabelled dataset. These two datasets are then combined into a larger dataset, which is used to train a final model.

While semi-supervised learning can significantly reduce data collection costs and increase accuracy, it comes with a risk of increasing bias in the data and model. Despite these risks, semi-supervised learning can sometimes be a viable solution. For example, let's say the cost of labelling millions of cat and dog pictures is too high for the case, but you have all the images available. You could label a thousand of each type, and the model could automatically label the rest. Your model would be based on both the labelled and auto-labelled data. This usually works best when there are few labels, and they're distinct.

GENERATIVE VERSUS PREDICTIVE AI

Generative AI refers to large pre-trained models that output texts, images, or sounds from user-provided prompts. The output is (potentially) unique and mimics human-generated content. It's based on the prompt and data used to train a large pre-trained model. Text-generating models such as OpenAI's GPT or Google's LaMDA are implementations of generative AI, also known as large language models.

Predictive AI comprises models that output one or more labels (prediction or classification) or numbers (regression or time series).

It includes:

- image building blocks: image classification, object detection and image segmentation
- tabular building blocks: prediction, regression, and forecast
- text building blocks: text classification, named entity recognition and intent analysis

An alternative and more accurate academic name for predictive AI is *discriminative AI*. However, "predictive" is clearer and less likely to be misunderstood.

GENERATIVE AI CAN ALSO PREDICT

Generative AI can also solve predictive problems. For example, ChatGPT can learn to classify texts through a few examples (few-shot learning) or no examples at all (zero-shot learning). The functionality might be the same, but there's a technical difference. Generative AI doesn't need you to train an algorithm that produces a model that it can then classify. Instead, the generative model gets the examples as a part of the prompt.

The upside of using generative models for predictive tasks is that they can be implemented immediately. However, there are downsides, such as:

- no way to calculate the expected performance through (for example) accuracy measures
- the generative model might provide an output that isn't part of the list of provided labels
- each prompt for output might affect future output

- generative models tend to "forget" the initial examples as there's a limit to how much prompting (or prompt input) they can remember

In this chapter we explored the core concept of AI as distinct from traditional information technology, based on its reliance on data and machine learning algorithms. We clarified the nuances of the terminology, like data and examples, and addressed the misconception that AI equates to human-like intelligence.

A clear, realistic understanding of AI is the first key to effectively apply this technology. As you will see throughout this book communication is crucial in AI and having a common language and the same definitions is necessary for successful implementation.

CHAPTER 3
AI BUILDING BLOCKS

Understanding the foundational building blocks of AI is crucial for newcomers to the domain. Once you grasp them, you can tackle any challenge by aligning it with the appropriate building blocks. This perspective simplifies your perception of AI and makes its application more straightforward and effective. The rest of the book will refer to these blocks by name. If you are already comfortable in the building blocks of AI, then you can skip or skim this chapter and come back to it if needed.

We can use the metaphor of an Italian kitchen to help conceptualise the relationship between AI building blocks, trained models, algorithms, and input data.

Think of AI building blocks as risotto, spaghetti carbonara, or polenta dishes. When faced with a problem, we select the building block we believe is the most useful. This is like how a chef chooses a suitable dish for a dinner.

To make a dish, you start with a recipe. In AI, algorithms are the recipes. A recipe is technically an algorithm, and our AI algorithms are based on the same common concepts. While variations and tweaks in the recipes may exist, they rely on the same mechanisms. A skilled chef (or data scientist) understands the reasoning behind the recipe and can adjust based on the circumstances while still producing an excellent outcome.

In AI, the data is like the ingredients you purchase for making a risotto. Just as in cooking, the quality of the ingredients (or data) can significantly impact the outcome. Better quality ingredients can lead to better results. A skilled chef using quality ingredients can create a better dish than a novice with subpar ingredients. The same principle applies in AI, where investing in high-quality data is more beneficial than focusing solely on modelling. Therefore, it's recommended to prioritise data over modelling when investing in AI.

The model is the final product, like the dish that's served. It represents the culmination of your hard work and allows you to evaluate the success of your efforts by testing and tasting its quality.

NO HOMEMADE PASTA

Many people opt for pre-made ingredients such as pasta, stock, and wine to save time and effort. Making pasta from scratch can be time-consuming and expensive, so purchasing it ready-made is a practical and sensible option. Similarly, in cooking and AI development, time and budget are limited resources, and investing in creating foundational models from scratch may not be the best option. Rather than relying on inventing new algorithms and models, maximising resources by using pre-existing models wherever possible is more effective.

An overview of building blocks

The building blocks in this table are archetypes and may undergo changes as technology advances.

Table	Vision	Language	Sound
Classification	classification	classification	classification
Regression	object detection	named entity recognition	audio generation
Forecasting	segmentation	intent analysis	
		sentiment analysis	
		writing text	
		text summarisation	

Table 3: Building blocks

Many people believe that working with different data types in AI requires specialisation and you can only work with one data type at a professional level. In my experience, this only applies to data scientists researching a particular data type. There's no need for someone building business solutions to specialise in one data type.

BUILDING BLOCKS

AI solutions are created using basic building blocks that are uniform. An AI building block is a fundamental concept of functionality defined by the input data required to train a model and the format in which the trained model outputs predictions. For example, the building block for image classification has images divided into categories as training data. The model produces a confidence score for each pre-defined category when classifying an image. This indicates the likelihood of the model correctly identifying the image as belonging to that category.

It's common to divide AI into building blocks, but the definition and division of these blocks vary. Some define the blocks in high-level abstract functionalities, such as "information processing" or "learning from data." Others base the divisions on the activities involved in building AI, such as "data collection" or "training models."

I divide the building blocks based on the input data and prediction output format to make them more objectively distinguishable and easier to understand and apply. This division also covers user cases for AI, as any proposed solution can be built using one or more building blocks.

If we divided AI into more abstract building blocks, such as "information processing" and "learning from data," there'd be too much room for subjective interpretation. This could hinder effective communication and shared understanding, essential for successful AI development. It's vital to maintain the advantages of using AI building blocks, including having a shared language and understanding among project participants, domain experts and designers, even those new to working with AI. Open-ended concepts such as "learning from data" could compromise this advantage.

In addition to establishing a shared language, AI building blocks offer the benefit of making the design process feel like playing with LEGO. You can connect models from different building blocks to create a modular AI solution.

Categorising the building blocks based on the type of data input is an easy way to estimate the costs of building an AI solution early on. Some blocks may require costly data, while others need easily accessible and pre-processed data. These details help you make informed decisions about the solution's scope. By anticipating the costs of each building block, you can avoid agreeing to small changes in the solution that may later be excessively expensive.

The blocks are divided into four main categories:

1. tabular
2. vision
3. language
4. sound

If you understand the twenty most common building blocks, you can solve almost any problem with AI. Keep in mind that AI development is fast-paced, and the building blocks may be updated and change over time.

The building blocks aren't directly equivalent to algorithms, and each building block can be constructed using a variety of algorithms. It doesn't necessarily matter what the specific underlying algorithm is (whether it's logistic regression, random forest, or a deep neural network). However, in some instances, such as in terms of explainability, the choice of algorithm may be significant. For example, deep learning-based algorithms provide little explainability, and decision-tree-based algorithms (such as Random Forest) provide high explainability.

LABELS AND FEATURES ARE FUNDAMENTAL TO AI BUILDING BLOCKS.

The *label* (or *target*) represents the desired answer that an AI model is trained to predict. If the AI is designed to recognise images of cats and dogs, the label would be "cat" or "dog" for each image. For text classification to sort emails, the labels could be "spam" or "not spam."

Features are the characteristics of the data we use to make predictions about the label. The AI algorithm uses features as the basis of its model. Some building blocks require specific features that are relevant to the task at hand. For example, in a bank loan default predictor, features could include the individual's age, income and prior history of failed payments. These features help the AI algorithm learn patterns and make accurate predictions.

In structured data, some building blocks have clearly defined features, such as in the default predictor example. However, for other building blocks, the features are implicitly learned by the model during training; for example, an image classifier that distinguishes between cats and dogs. The model doesn't explicitly define the features it uses to make this distinction. Instead, it discovers these features through pattern recognition and internalising relationships between the input data and output labels. While it's possible to extrapolate these features, it can be challenging and technically demanding.

TABULAR BUILDING BLOCKS

Tabular or *structured* data is what we find in Excel sheets or databases. This data type is organised into rows and columns, which can be labelled as features or labels based on their usage. It's versatile and can be used for various purposes, such as predicting risks, forecasting and predictive maintenance. The fundamental building blocks in the tabular data category are classification, regression, and forecasting.

CLASSIFICATION

Classification is a technique used to categorise entities based on their features. A classification model takes input data features and predicts a class or category based on those features.

For example, consider credit card fraud detection. In this scenario, the input data is a list of past credit card transactions labelled as either fraud or non-fraud. These labels are the classes the model aims to predict. The credit card transaction data may appear as follows

Label	Amount	Card owner ID	Transaction time	Merchant ID
fraud	53	8473682	5 Nov 2021 08.40	43868504
not_fraud	60	9484727	5 Nov 2021 10.31	21337316
not_fraud	200	9583734	5 Nov 2021 12.29	81532386

Table 4: Classification

The label represents the target variable we aim to predict, while the remaining columns represent the features. In the case of credit card fraud detection, the label can be "fraud" or "non-fraud."

Once the model is trained, we can use it to make predictions based on new transaction data, which consists of features such as transaction amount, location, and time. The model returns a prediction based on these features, indicating whether the transaction is fraudulent or not.

A typical prediction would appear as follows:

Amount	Card owner ID	Transaction time	Merchant ID
140	8473682	8 Nov 2021 07.26	82217758

Table 5: Data query

Prediction output (confidence score):

Fraud: 78%Not fraud: 22%

After analysing the input features, the model outputs the predicted label and its corresponding probability. This is often called the *confidence score*. In scenarios like credit card fraud detection, where there's only one possible correct answer, the sum of predictions will always be 100%.

While the number of labels can range from two to millions, a larger number of data records (rows) is often required for comparable accuracy. Furthermore, it's possible to create models that perform multi-classification, where multiple labels can be true simultaneously. In such cases, the sum of the likelihood of predicted labels can be greater than 100%.

If you're interested in building a tabular classification model, I recommend downloading a well-known dataset focusing on survivors of the Titanic disaster. This can be used to predict the probability of survival based on features such as age, gender, and class. The data can be downloaded from Kaggle, a great place to find data for AI problems.

REGRESSION

Regression is a tabular-based building block, resembling classification in many ways. The primary difference is that regression produces a numerical output as a prediction instead of a class. Consequently, the training data label must also be a number. An example of regression is forecasting the price of a house. This numerical output affects how we approach output confidence.

Regression also comes in simple formats. You might recall plotting a line or a function between points on a graph in school maths. With this modelling approach, the computer does the same thing; it calculates the best-fit function through the provided data points. With this function, you can input new data and receive a numerical output.

A model for predicting house prices might incorporate features such as the number of rooms, postcode, square footage and year of construction. Training data for such a model could take on the following form:

Label	Features			
Price	Postcode	Number of rooms	m^2	Year built
€250k	2000	yellow	190	1990
€140k	2200	red	140	1960
€350k	2900	white	230	1930

Table 6: Labels and features

When querying the model for the price of a new house, the input data might resemble the following:

Postcode	Number of rooms	m^2	Year built
2200	4	172	1962

Table 7: Input data

Prediction output:

The output could look like this:

Prediction: €231,821

95% prediction interval: €177,878-€287,184

A regression model simultaneously predicts a numerical value and a corresponding range of certainty. For instance, there may be a 95% likelihood that the correct outcome falls within the range of €177,878 to €287,184). Narrower intervals are preferable, as they indicate greater confidence in the model's prediction.

Another application of regression is in agriculture, where it can be used to forecast crop output. A regression model can estimate the likely yield using various features of a given field, such as current crop height, rainfall levels and weather forecasts.

Regression models have also demonstrated impressive results in predicting sales and marketing campaign outcomes.

FORECASTING

Forecasting using AI is like regression, but with the added element of time. Forecasting is also often referred to as a *time series*. In forecasting, the input data is a historical record of events with a number as the label. The output is future events with a number for each time interval.

Let's say we want to predict how much ice cream will be sold in a specific area over a certain period, accounting for multiple sales outlets.

The training data might take on the following format:

Label	Time series ID	Timestamp	Features				
Ice cream sales	ID	Date	Weather	°C	Store#	Postcode
15	12939	24 Aug 2021	sunny	27	2	1990
24	49282	24 Aug 2021	rain	28	4	1960
18	39482	26 Aug 2021	cloudy	30	2	1930

Table 8: Training data

The label refers to what we're attempting to forecast – in this instance, the quantity of ice cream sold. If we were to graph this data, the label would appear on the y-axis.

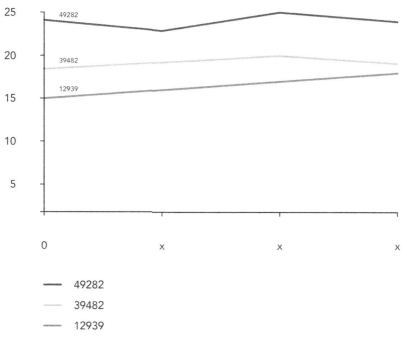

Figure 3: Forecasting sales

Each event, such as the quantity of ice cream sold on a given day, has its own unique identifier, known as the *time series ID*.

As with regression and classification, the features are the variables used to predict the label value. In this case, factors like weather have an impact on ice cream sales. Selecting the appropriate features for a model is referred to as *feature engineering*. The result of a forecasting model might appear as follows:

Label	Timestamp	Features	
Predicted_sales	Date	Weather_forecast	Degrees_forecast
23.34	1 Sept 2021	sunny	27
18.22	2 Sept 2021	sunny	28
15.03	3 Sept 2021	rain	24

Table 9: Forecasting Model

We've generated a forecasted sales value for each date using meteorological data as features. An obvious limitation of this model is the accuracy of weather predictions. Forecasting solutions often have a limited ability when it comes to predicting too far in the future, as some features can only be known for a short period ahead.

Examples of forecasting use cases include:

- Traffic forecasting: Transportation and logistics companies predict traffic flow. This allows them to plan for optimal routes, schedules, and staffing levels.
- Supply chain management: Forecasting models can help businesses anticipate future product demand. This allows them to optimise their inventory levels and production schedules.
- Energy consumption forecasting: Energy companies use forecasting models to predict future energy demands. This helps them manage their supply and plan for maintenance and upgrades.

What the use cases above have in common is that they contain a time element.

Forecasting and regression may seem similar, but regression deals with onetime or standalone events while forecasting is better for continuous timeframes. Forecasting is your best building block if you're working with a continuous timeframe.

While simple projections based on past data may work in some cases, AI-based forecasting can be a better choice when comparable time frames can't be predicted with a trendline. For example, if your sales depend on factors such as marketing efforts, market trends and weather, a simple projection based on last year's sales plus a fixed percentage increase might not be accurate enough. In such cases, AI-based forecasting can help you consider multiple variables and their complex interactions, allowing you to make more accurate predictions.

In tabular models, it's possible to incorporate other types of data, such as text or images, through a process called *embedding*. This involves converting the text or image into a list of numbers (also known as a *vector*), which can be used as a feature in the model.

Large language or image models are used to perform the embedding process, which converts the raw data into vectors. These vectors represent the data in an abstract manner, and their distance from each other can be calculated through simple subtractions. For example, the vectors for "cat" and "dog" will be closer than those for "cat" and "house." Using this method, the algorithm can consider how text or images impact the prediction.

VISION BUILDING BLOCKS

Vision is data in the form of images or a series of images (video). Building blocks are used to identify objects within images, classify them, and segregate them from their backgrounds. For example, in self-driving cars, vision-based AI identifies objects in images, such as pedestrians and other vehicles, by placing small bounding boxes around them.

CLASSIFICATION

The initial building block in computer vision is image classification. This involves predicting the pre-defined classes for a given image. Basically, this building block receives an image as input and identifies it as belonging to one of the pre-defined categories or labels for which the model has been trained. The model must discover how to recognise the visual features in the image that correspond to specific classes or labels.

When a new image is fed into the image classification model, it analyses the image and assigns it to the most appropriate label or category. The confidence score provided by the model reflects how confident the model is in its classification. Higher scores indicate greater certainty.

A model trained for classifying cats and dogs could get an output like this:

Figure 4: Classifying cats and dogs

And return an output like this:

dog: 94%cat: 6%

In multi-classification models, each image can be associated with multiple correct labels. With multi-classification, we can achieve more fine-grained predictions that better reflect the complexities of the real world. For example, a picture of a car could be labelled as "vehicle," "automobile," and "transportation." This allows for more accurate and detailed predictions for a variety of use cases, from image recognition to natural language processing.

Sorting images into folders that correspond to their labels is all that's required for collecting data for classification. This simple process makes labelling data for classification the most cost-effective building block in the vision data type.

OBJECT DETECTION

Object detection goes beyond image classification by identifying both the type of object in an image and its precise location within the frame.

In the context of a self-driving car, an image classification building block could only provide information about whether a pedestrian or another vehicle is present in the image. In contrast, object detection would predict the appearance and position of the object in the image. This information is crucial for the self-driving car to decide when to stop or continue driving. For example, if a pedestrian is on the pavement, there would be no need for the car to stop. However, if the pedestrian is on the road, the car needs to take action to avoid a collision. The vehicle can make an informed decision by using object detection to locate the pedestrian's position precisely.

In this scenario, the input to the model would still be an image, but the output would consist of bounding boxes that enclose the identified objects. These bounding boxes are rectangles containing information about the objects' coordinates and size.

The raw output from the image above could be something like this:

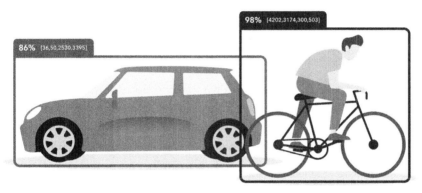

Figure 5: Classifying objects

person: 98% [4202,3174,300,503]car: 86% [36,50,2530,3395]

The output shows the prediction confidence level and the coordinates for the bounding box placing the object.

Collecting data for object detection models is more labour-intensive than for classification models. To train an object detection model, the data must be labelled with bounding boxes that outline the objects to be detected. This means drawing bounding boxes around the objects in every image in the training dataset, a process that can take five to ten times longer per image than preparing data for classification models.

Both paid (for example, Labelbox, Prodigy and hasty.ai) and free (for example, CVAT and LabelStudio) software tools are available to make labelling tasks easier. Nevertheless, object detection requires more work than classification.

Try classification first

Even if object detection is the preferred building block for an AI solution, it can be beneficial to start with image classification to gain experience and insight before investing in collecting data for object detection.

In a recent project, we used satellite images to identify buildings with solar panels and cooling towers. Initially, we started with an image classification model. However, a satellite image doesn't automatically zoom in on any specific rooftop. That meant that solar panels or cooling towers on neighbouring buildings signalled a positive prediction. There was a substantial risk of false positives for the presence of cooling towers in the wrong buildings.

Starting with image classification was a good decision, as it allowed us to quickly collect and train on data and gain insights for developing the object detection model. We also discovered that the classification model struggled to identify solar panels on buildings with dark windows. This experience enabled us to collect more training data for the object detection model and be aware of potential challenges when labelling data. We recognised that if the AI made the mistake of confusing windows for solar panels, human annotators would likely make the same mistake. Based on that, we could ensure that extra care was taken not to label windows as solar panels.

IMAGE SEGMENTATION

Image segmentation identifies the precise boundary of an object in an image. This is useful for applications such as calculating the area of fields or buildings from aerial footage and for mapping organs in CT scans in the healthcare industry.

Figure 6: Object outlines

The input for this method is an image, and the output is the exact outline of the identified objects. However, collecting data for segmentation can be a time-consuming and expensive process. Manually marking the boundary of an object with a mouse can take a significant amount of time, especially for irregularly shaped objects. Therefore, segmentation is considered the most resource-intensive and costly image-building block.

IMAGE SIMILARITY

The image similarity building block aims to predict how closely related two images are by comparing their embedded vectors from a pre-trained image model. Unlike other vision models, no model training is required for image similarity. Instead, a pre-trained model can be downloaded and used to generate similarity scores between two images in a few minutes. The model's output is a number between 0 and 1, where 1 represents a perfect match between the images.

Image similarity is particularly useful when dealing with many possible classes to compare to the input image. For example, in a product identification system with 100,000 different products in the catalogue, collecting sufficient training data for each product to make a classification model would be impractical. Using image similarity, a single image of each product is needed to create a functional solution. Although the accuracy may not be as high as a classification model, the cost savings in data collection make it an attractive option.

In vision AI, we have four supervised building blocks:

- classification
- object detection
- segmentation
- similarity

Data labelling becomes more time-consuming and expensive in this order. As a result, it's best to attempt classification and then object detection *before* segmentation to solve a problem.

When deciding which building block to use, consider the value of knowing the positions and shapes of objects in images. Object detection or segmentation should be a priority if this information is important. However, if inexpensive data is a priority, image classification is a better option.

Similarity is an unsupervised method that's simple to use. It's a great choice when you need to make direct comparisons between images or when you have limited training data.

LANGUAGE BUILDING BLOCKS

Natural language processing is dedicated to analysing written text input in the language data category. It has various applications, such as chatbots, categorising emails, identifying keywords, and generating natural language.

The most prevalent examples are AI-based translation, exemplified by Google Translate, and *question answering*, which involves training AI to answer questions such as "How tall is the Eiffel tower?"

The approach to language processing has recently evolved dramatically. While older methods entailed constructing local dictionaries from the words in the text, the current approach employs pre-trained models that already possess a significant representation of language structure.

CLASSIFICATION

Text classification is the simplest building block in the language category. Its objective is to categorise text into pre-defined classes or categories.

For example, suppose you wanted to build a text classifier for a company's incoming messages. Text classification could speed up customer dialogue by routing messages to the appropriate department. The messages could be intended for the sales or support department, but you may not know which until you read them. With text classification, incoming messages can be automatically categorised for their appropriate departments, streamlining communication.

One possible way to represent labelled text data for training a text classification model is as follows:

Label	Text
Support	Hi, can you help me figure out how the product works?
Sales	When can you deliver my order?
Support	I can't remember my login credentials. Can you help me?
Sales	Is the price set in stone or open for negotiation?

Tabel 10: Labelled text data

41

Text classification is a relatively fast process for labelling new data because it involves sorting and grouping texts based on pre-defined labels. When using the trained model to predict the label of a new text, the output may look something like this:

Input text: "I'd like to order five units for next week. Is that possible?"

Prediction output:

sales: 85%support: 15%

Text classification has a wide range of use cases, including email and document categorisation or sorting. For example, email providers can use text classification algorithms to classify incoming emails as spam, important, or social.

Paperflow used text classification to recognise different types of financial documents, including invoices, receipts, credit notes and account statements. Understanding what type of financial document, the model was looking at first could help the model make better predictions. For example, finding the price on an invoice line makes the line easy to identify. However, if an order didn't have prices on the lines, this wouldn't be a useful indicator.

This classification process was particularly helpful in identifying different data field entities on invoices and account statements, streamlining document processing, and improving overall efficiency.

NAMED ENTITY RECOGNITION

Named entity recognition (NER) identifies specific entities within texts, such as product descriptions, invoices, emails, or contracts. It's useful for recognising names, dates, addresses and amounts. For example, NER could extract customer names and addresses from contracts. In email processing, NER could be used to extract information, such as sender names and email addresses.

However, collecting data for NER can be significantly more time-consuming than text classification, as it involves reading through training data and marking words in the text with a digital marker.

Additionally, defining labels for NER can be challenging and imprecise, as people may have different definitions of the same entity. For example, the definition of a "location" might differ from person to person, making it challenging to label consistently.

In NER, we typically have several labels defined for a solution. Examples of entities in natural language could be identifying names, locations, job functions, dates or amounts, or customer numbers.

Although NER may appear like conventional text searching, the functions differ significantly. While both search for specific entities, the traditional search takes a text string such as "Paris" and finds exact or nearly exact matches in texts or documents. NER goes beyond the surface level of text and leverages contextual information to identify entities.

For example, you could use NER to find all instances of city names within a given text, even if it doesn't have an exhaustive list of all possible city names. NER uses contextual information to guess the entity referred to, just as humans would. This is particularly useful when dealing with complex data where entity names might be ambiguous or with entities that can refer to multiple things. For instance, "Frank" can refer to several cities, but it can also be a person's name, or even an adjective meaning "direct." NER helps identify the correct entity in context, providing more accurate and reliable results than a traditional text search.

The NER building block in AI relies heavily on pre-trained models to identify entities based on contextual clues. For example, in the sentence "I'm going to visit Havana next week," the pre-trained model would identify "Havana" as a city due to its contextual position. In contrast, in the sentence "I was drinking Havana all night and now my head hurts," the pre-trained model would identify "Havana" as a type of rum.

In our work with Paperflow, we used NER to extract key data fields, such as the sender of an invoice, dates, amounts, and product lines. However, specific entities like invoice numbers were challenging to predict using natural language alone, as they often consisted of a few digits placed without contextual clues. Conversely, total amounts were more readily identified by contextual clues, such as a preceding word like "amount."

INTENT ANALYSIS

Intent analysis, recognition, or classification refers to the process of determining the meaning of a text. Since longer texts may have several meanings, this building block can produce a list of results found in the input text.

Chatbots provide an example of intent analysis. When you ask a chatbot a question, the input is a short text string, and the model attempts to match the correct labels (intents) to which the chatbot can respond.

Text classification and intent analysis can seem similar. In both cases, you have a set of labels or categories into which you want to classify texts. The main difference is in the type of labels used. In text classification, labels are more general and straightforward, such as categories or topics, while in intent analysis, labels represent the specific intentions or purposes of the text.

The difference lies in the granularity of the labels and the task's purpose. While text classification aims to group texts based on general topics, intent analysis aims to identify the specific purpose or goal of, for example, a user's message.

SENTIMENT ANALYSIS

Sentiment analysis involves categorising the emotion or mood expressed in a text with a pre-defined set of sentiments. It can be used in customer service software to identify quickly if a support message from a client is happy or angry. It's also commonly used by marketing and PR systems that scan the web for articles and measure the sentiment generated by a brand's mention.

AI-based sentiment analysis can predict context-specific sentiments. For example, a thirty-minute delay may not be a significant issue for an airline, but it could be unacceptable in a coffee shop.

Modern sentiment analysis can interpret the overall tone of a text and recognise positive mentions of a brand in an otherwise negative context. That could be a news article on climate change where a brand in question is producing windmills.

Text or sentence similarity is a fundamental building block that measures the degree of similarity between two pieces of text. It operates like image similarity, comparing two images to determine their similarity. Text similarity is often unsupervised, meaning it doesn't require prior training.

The input-to-text similarity is the two texts that need to be compared, and the output is a value between 0 and 1, with 1 indicating a perfect match.

For example, suppose you want to identify if a customer's question has been asked before to see how the problem was solved at that time. You can use text similarity to compare a new customer inquiry with previous ones. The advantage of AI-based similarity is that the questions can differ in wording and still seem similar.

An example could be:

Question 1: How do I fix my coffee machine if the grinder is blocked?

Question 2: My coffee beans aren't going through the mill. What should I do?

Although the wording is significantly different, the meaning remains the same, and the use of this AI building block is still perceived as similar. Text similarity makes it possible to compare numerous texts quickly, and it's ideal for many search-related tasks.

In recent years, AI-based text generation has made impressive advances, particularly with the development of substantial pre-trained models like OpenAI's ChatGPT and Googles PaLM2, which have garnered significant attention.

These LLMs can now easily generate text by a user prompting them to do so. Such text generation models are typically pre-trained since they require vast amounts of data and entail enormous training costs.

As an illustration, let's consider a short example of how data science projects often fail, as generated by ChatGPT in response to the prompt, "Write a short example of why data science projects often fail."

The model response:

There are many reasons why data science projects may fail. One common reason is a lack of clear goals and objectives. Without a clear understanding of what the project is trying to achieve, it can be difficult to decide which data to collect and analyse and how to interpret the results.

Another reason data science projects may fail is due to a lack of resources, such as insufficient funding or a lack of skilled personnel. This can lead to delays in the project, or a lack of the necessary tools and technology to complete the project effectively.

Another issue that can lead to the failure of a data science project is poor communication and collaboration among team members. If team members aren't on the same page, it can be difficult to make progress and achieve the desired outcomes.

Finally, a lack of data quality can also be a major challenge for data science projects. If the data being used is incomplete, inaccurate, or not relevant to the project, it can be difficult to draw meaningful insights and make effective decisions.

Although the outcomes of AI-based text generation may appear remarkable, it has limitations. The primary challenge is that while the generated text reads as comprehensive and fluent English, it may contain a mixture of accurate and inaccurate statements. There's currently no effective method to test its validity, making it challenging to use for production purposes.

This difficulty arises due to the vast amounts of data used to train text generation models, which is predominantly sourced from the internet and may not have been thoroughly fact-checked. As a result, it can be challenging to determine the accuracy and reliability of the generated text.

AI models have demonstrated the ability to produce well-written code and have even been used by data scientists at Todai for generating code. With ChatGPT, developers can prompt the model to perform a specific task, such as "Write a Python script that opens all files in folder X and adds the file content to a list" and ChatGPT returns the code as a result.

The result of that looks like this:

```python
import os

# Define the path to folder X
folder_path = 'path/to/folder/X'   # Replace 'path/to/folder/X' with the actual path to your folder

# Initialize an empty list to hold the contents of the files
file_contents = []

# Loop through each file in the directory
for filename in os.listdir(folder_path):
    # Construct the full file path
    file_path = os.path.join(folder_path, filename)

    # Check if it is a file
    if os.path.isfile(file_path):
        # Open the file and read its contents
        with open(file_path, 'r') as file:
            content = file.read()
            # Add the content to the list
            file_contents.append(content)

# Now file_contents list contains the contents of all the files in the folder
print(file_contents)
```

Figure 7: Python task script

In addition to generating code, ChatGPT can also optimise code provided to it. Surprisingly, ChatGPT often produces more concise, effective, and easily readable code than humans.

The quality and accuracy of the generated code can vary depending on the language. For example, pre-trained models in Danish (my native language) aren't as advanced as English ones, making AI-based text generation less useful.

SUMMARISING TEXT

Text summarisation involves reducing the length of a longer text while retaining its most important points. It enables you to extract critical information from lengthy texts more efficiently.

This can be achieved through a variety of techniques. *Extractive summarisation* involves selecting and condensing essential sentences from the original text. *Abstractive summarisation* involves generating a new text that accurately captures the critical points of the original text in a condensed format.

SOUND

The sound data type includes the building blocks that enable your Google Home or Amazon Alexa to understand voice commands through speech-to-text models. This model first converts the sound of your voice into text. It's then interpreted, generating an appropriate response, much like a chatbot.

Recently, a new type of model called Wave2Vec has emerged. This can classify speech directly without an intermediate speech-to-text step. Wave2Vec works by embedding sounds into vectors, making grouping, and comparing them more efficiently. A practical application of Wave2Vec is in comparing songs. By classifying the sounds of different songs, Wave2Vec can group them into similar categories, which can help generate accurate music recommendations.

AUDIO CLASSIFICATION

Audio classification enables you to input an audio clip that's then classified into pre-defined categories. Like other classification building blocks, the training data for this model is organised into groups.

I've used audio classification to identify coughs from pigs in barns to determine if they suffer from pneumonia. This approach worked well, even with limited training data. While there may be limited use cases for audio classification, it's a low-cost and low-effort solution.

MULTIMODAL BUILDING BLOCKS

Multimodal building blocks combine a variety of data types, taking one input and producing another output. For example:

- **Text-to-image** accepts a prompt text as an input (for example, "an image of a teddy bear riding a skateboard in Times Square") and generates a corresponding visual representation. Examples of such models include Dall-e 2 and Stable Diffusion.
- **Image-to-text** takes an image as input and attempts to output a suitable caption.
- **Text-to-speech** takes a text and reads it aloud in the most human way possible. Some model outputs have proved to be almost impossible to distinguish from natural human speech.
- **Speech-to-text** (*speech recognition*) converts written text into spoken words, striving to make the output sound as human as possible. It's become increasingly valuable in recent years, as some model outputs are almost indistinguishable from natural human speech.

You can combine building blocks to solve a more complex problem. It's like building with LEGO. If you have a substantial task that a single building block can't solve, you can break it down into smaller bits. You do that until each subtask can be solved with a single building block.

Let's say you're an insurance company that wants to detect fraudulent claims received via email. The first step is to identify the claimant, which you can do with a named entity recognition model to recognise their name, social security ID or policy number. Once the claimant is identified, a text classifier can be used to assess the likelihood of fraud based on the claim description.

However, it may be necessary to use additional data to judge the fraud risk accurately. Factors such as the claimant's length of time as a customer and the number of claims made in the last ten years are relevant features that should be included in a tabular classification model.

This approach can help improve fraud detection and mitigate potential losses.

You can combine this by taking the result from the text classifier and using that as a data point in the tabular model, as shown in the illustration.

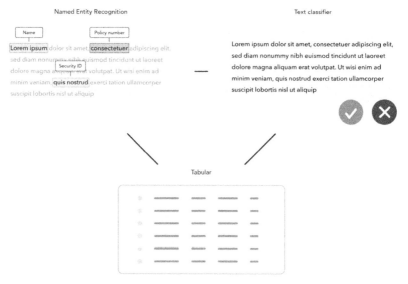

Figure 8: Tabular classification model

Another example is the ice cream store case discussed earlier. Here, the ice cream sales prediction had local traffic as an input to the model. Local traffic was counted in real-time with live feeds from highway cameras. An object detection model was deployed to count the cars.

As you gain experience with AI, you'll become better at identifying the appropriate building block for a potential solution.

In addition, in helping you match AI capabilities with business problems, these building blocks simplify communication. Take the time to explain the relevant building blocks to stakeholders involved in AI solutions. This will make it simpler for you to clarify your choices.

CHAPTER 4

PREPARING YOUR ORGANISATION FOR REAPING THE BENEFITS OF AI

In a 2022 survey, only 24% of Danish companies claimed to use AI, which was incorrect.[1] The fact is that companies use AI to varying degrees.

What does it mean to use AI?

- Do you need to develop your own AI models?
- Does it suffice to use off-the-shelf AI tools?
- Or is it enough that an employee uses a tool or a service that includes an AI module?

Today, most IT services use AI technology. For example, your email server has an AI spam filter, and your email client operates an AI-based spell checker. Your antivirus uses AI to identify malware; when you search on your browser, you interact with AI modules.

Moreover, your business management systems probably have AI embedded, too. For example, your customer relationship management system uses AI to suggest leads to prioritise and estimate the expected revenue from your current pipeline. Your enterprise resource planning system might read payable invoices, prefill data fields, and propose the correct book-keeping account. Your project management system may include an AI-based feature to estimate resource requirements.

With the emergence of ChatGPT and similar solutions, AI has become easily accessible. Employees may use it to solve everyday tasks without consulting management, reading guidelines, or understanding the consequences.

Some try to ban ChatGPT but soon find out that isn't possible. Recently, a data protection officer from a large corporation told me she'd completely banned ChatGPT in her company. I responded that I was helping one of their software providers build ChatGPT into their software and that software was probably not the only software getting an LLM built into it.

It's highly likely that you and your colleagues interact with AI daily and provide it with data. Sometimes it is apparent that AI is used, and sometimes it is not.

The discussion above matters for two reasons.

First, AI is already heavily involved in decision-making processes. Companies can choose to leave it at that, with most employees unaware of AI's role and how it operates. Or they can choose to upskill their staff to understand the systems they use.

Second, everything done digitally becomes training data for AI, which has an impact elsewhere. Therefore, it's advantageous to understand how and where data is used. For example, updating a delivery date in a project management system can affect future project predictions. A model could be designed to predict the likelihood of a client accepting a sales proposal using sales history entered by sales reps into the enterprise resource planning system (ERP) as training data. If employees understand the basis of AI, they'll also understand how data affects their jobs. That will give them an incentive to improve data quality. They'll realise that accuracy and discipline will greatly impact upon them, their colleagues, and the organisation's overall performance.

Adopting AI can fail if, instead of focusing on problems you must resolve and considering how it could help, you assume it's enough to make it part of your processes. Below is a real-life case study. (I've altered the names and anonymised the activities to maintain confidentiality.)

Knowledge Corp is a consulting company. Its staff have university degrees (including in engineering) and years of experience working with advanced statistics and using algorithms that overlap with those used in AI. With their background, you'd expect that top management's decision to adopt AI, for both internal solutions and service offerings, would be a walk in the park.

Knowledge Corp hired a small team of data scientists, asking them to find the problems that AI could solve.

Their activities quickly became a nuisance to the rest of the organisation. It was unclear what exactly the data scientists were looking for. As everyone was busy with their daily tasks, serving customers and billing hours, there was little time for talking to data scientists.

After a couple of frustrating engagements, management pushed for other departments to engage, and they identified a few promising opportunities.

Unfortunately, the necessary data for these projects wasn't readily accessible. Extensive analysis and preparation were required before any AI modelling could begin. Acquiring, storing and cleaning the data took significantly longer than anticipated.

As time passed, the Knowledge Corp staff started asking questions about the AI initiative. The team had not been able to demonstrate a single AI solution. They were expensive, and more and more Knowledge Corp staff members asked, "Why are we even doing this?"

This is a common scenario. How do you implement AI effectively and avoid the pitfalls that Knowledge Corp encountered? There are strategies you can use for successfully managing a data science team and begin integrating AI even if you haven't yet hired data scientists.

Adopting AI means you can:

- Develop the ability to spot potential opportunities for AI solutions that may have substantial value

- Determine which opportunities should be built or bought
- Identify solutions to significant challenges that were previously considered unresolvable
- Understand which competencies are required and which process to follow when solving problems with AI

DOMAIN EXPERTS

The term *domain expert* refers to a *subject matter expert* (SME) with specialised knowledge in a particular field. In AI, this term is used more broadly to include individuals with expertise in any area that can be leveraged to develop AI solutions. This includes, for instance, cashiers, doctors, and salespeople who have valuable insight into customer interaction, disease and patient relations, and the sales process, respectively.

Being a domain expert doesn't require a high level of education or being recognised as an authority figure in your field. Even a child in kindergarten is a domain expert if their knowledge can help predict afternoon napping patterns.

KNOWLEDGE DRIVES DEMAND

The primary objective of adopting AI is to meet business needs. It isn't about inventing or creating demand where it doesn't exist. Corporations have ample opportunities to enhance the value of their products, operations, and processes through AI, but without genuine demand, this potential value will remain untapped. Learning about AI will help you find the critical bottlenecks it can address and avoid useless projects.

IT'S NOT ABOUT HIRING TECHNICIANS FIRST

The individuals responsible for and involved in budgets, productivity, and business processes need knowledge and insight. They need to understand what AI is (and isn't) and know the fundamental building blocks.

A basic understanding of the building blocks enables people across the organisation to identify the most promising opportunities for AI. Once understanding and awareness exist across the organisation, everything else falls into place.

When considering the adoption of AI, it may be tempting to limit upskilling efforts to technical team members alone. This approach may appear faster, less costly, and less disruptive. However, this is a recipe for failure. Everyone involved needs to upskill for the best results, regardless of their position in the organisation.

If AI knowledge is only prevalent among the data science, AI, IT, or digitalisation teams, the organisation will experience suboptimal business results or no benefits at all. Knowledge Corp invested heavily in recruiting a data science team within the IT department, but the payoff didn't materialise until they'd educated hundreds of individuals across the organisation about AI.

WHY THE ENCAPSULATED AND TECHNICAL APPROACH FAILS

There are several reasons why the initial Knowledge Corp approach didn't work.

Firstly, getting ideas and spotting the potential for AI is best done by the staff who understand everyday business problems.

These individuals are subject-matter experts. For example, salespeople (especially the sales manager) possess valuable insights into the challenges associated with revenue forecasting. The administration team is well-versed in how manual bookkeeping processes are time-consuming. The factory floor staff are knowledgeable about daily safety risks. This insight can be leveraged to identify solution opportunities when combined with an understanding of AI principles and building blocks.

It takes significantly more time and effort to educate a few AI experts about every aspect of the organisation – often an impossible task – than to teach the organisation about the capabilities of AI. The objective isn't to turn everyone into a data scientist but to introduce them to AI concepts.

I'm not suggesting that data scientists and AI experts shouldn't acquire domain knowledge. However, investing effort in spreading awareness about AI is more effective when the goal is to demonstrate how it can be helpful before you begin building a solution. For example, a data science department leader recently said, "Give us a need for an AI solution, and we will deliver on it."

This approach leads to a stalemate. Business divisions are unaware of the possibilities offered by AI, so they don't request such solutions. Meanwhile, AI experts are either idle or attempting to create demand independently. The paradox is that these organisations possess significant potential to address internal issues and enhance their products and services through AI. Still, nothing happens due to a lack of widespread awareness and understanding.

Secondly, there's always resistance to new technology.

People tend to be more hesitant to adopt something they know little about – and they don't want to be among the first if uncertain. When adopting AI, there are three contact points where users might create resistance.

1. When attempting to validate potential uses for AI. Domain experts need to be involved in assessing the possible initiatives. However, if they lack prior knowledge of AI, they feel inadequate and view most ideas as a waste of time.
2. The discovery phase is when the solution is being scoped and designed.
3. During the implementation phase. Users may struggle to comprehend the objective if AI is presented solely as a technology-focused initiative.

Consider the scenario where you want to develop a forecasting system. The first step is to determine the value it can offer to users. Is the outcome worth the investment? Next, you need to collaborate with future users to determine how the system should function with their work.

Once the forecasting system is built, it must be implemented. This involves training users to input data into the system and interpret and act on its output. At both stages, there's a risk of resistance from users who are busy performing their job duties and may perceive the project as a disruption. They would rather serve customers than waste their time on an internal project.

Allowing people to become familiar with AI before introducing it can transform resistance into enthusiasm. It's remarkable how something so simple as a one-day introduction to AI can ignite interest, energy, and creativity. It can take almost no time until a pipeline of promising opportunities emerges where previously IT had been considered inapplicable.

This approach isn't only advantageous for fostering innovation by generating more ideas. It also benefits the data science department. In Knowledge Corp, the data scientists transitioned from being viewed as a disruptive nuisance to being hailed as superheroes. This transformation was achieved through a company-wide AI briefing initiative.

Thirdly, the engagement of subject-matter experts improves when they understand what AI entails.

If you're building a model to predict delays in construction plans, you need the current project planners (the domain experts) to identify the most decisive variables. If they understand the basics of AI and what they're trying to help you achieve, they'll do it more effectively and enthusiastically. Getting to the bottom of what was previously considered unsolvable business problems is much easier when the subject-matter experts are familiar with AI.

AI IS BOTTOM-UP

AI's success works from the bottom up. It can't be preached or enforced from the top down. Despite this, many companies are hesitant to embrace this approach. Some fear discussing AI will create anxiety and resistance, but the opposite is true. They also worry that if too many people learn about AI, they won't be able to control how it's adopted and used.

Limiting AI capabilities to a few technical experts is counterproductive. AI isn't solely a technology that organisations purchase or use to build solutions. It's also an essential technology that rapidly infiltrates IT systems. Adopting AI as an organisational capability will help you identify business needs that were previously considered unsolvable with traditional IT. Any management team should welcome such a situation.

As AI becomes more accessible, easier to implement and use, and more affordable, it can be adopted without costly technical resources.

HOW DO YOU TEACH AI?

You might believe AI is too complicated a technology to teach employees in finance, marketing, R&D, production, logistics, HR or sales. You may hesitate to remove individuals from their duties and place them in a classroom for training.

None of these concerns are justified.

The objective isn't to educate people on AI technical details, such as how neural networks operate or the mathematics. It's more efficient to teach the building blocks, the adoption strategies presented in this chapter, and the tools described below. It's not about transforming subject-matter experts into data scientists. Instead, it enables them to identify potential critical issues in their everyday tasks that only AI can help resolve.

BRIDGE THE GAP OF IGNORANCE.

The goal is to bridge the gap of ignorance between data scientists and subject matter experts. The most efficient and effective way to do this is through AI training that uses domain-specific cases. For example, if you work with farmers, you could demonstrate how to predict crop growth. Or, if you work with an insurance company, you can show them how to detect fraud. During training sessions, encourage participants to build models using their own data with tools like Teachable-Machine. Building their first model by collecting data, training, testing, and analysing the model's accuracy is critical to the learning process. This approach helps learning stick better than generic examples and often sparks new ideas.

Now that ChatGPT has made AI available to everyone, many people already have some insight into how it works. When participants say, "Is that it? Is that all AI is?" during training, they've grasped the principles.

TO ADOPT OR NOT TO ADOPT ISN'T A CHOICE

In recent years, many organisations have debated whether to adopt AI. This question is based on two misconceptions. The first is that adopting AI involves building and training models, which is expensive and time-consuming. The second is that you have a choice. It is not about whether to adopt AI but whether to adopt it *successfully*.

A TECHNOLOGY FOR SOLVING BUSINESS PROBLEMS

AI is a technology and the umbrella label for various methods that use examples rather than instructions. If you're not IT-savvy, it can be challenging to understand how it works. That's why companies often rely on their IT department to implement it. Data engineers and data scientists are then recruited to help support these efforts.

But what exactly do data engineers and data scientists do?

They code.

Even though almost perfect solutions are available in the market, IT people often say, "We can just as easily code that from scratch."

This phenomenon is known as the *not invented here* (NIH) syndrome. If a standard solution doesn't fit perfectly, some organisations create a custom solution instead of slightly modifying the requirements

Sometimes, developing a solution from scratch is necessary, but this should be the exception rather than the rule. However, the NIH syndrome is more common in the AI field than in other areas of IT. The main reason is the knowledge gap between technical staff and subject matter experts, making it difficult for the latter to map their business needs to IT solutions.

The media's hype of AI exaggerates this knowledge gap as a futuristic technology that will change the world. As a result, AI is often perceived as challenging to comprehend. But like getting a driver's licence doesn't require extensive knowledge about cars, using AI doesn't mean you need deep technical expertise. Instead, it involves identifying the AI tools for your needs and learning how to use them safely and effectively. If we took a technical-only approach to AI implementation, only experts in the field could use it, which is like thinking only mechanics and auto-engineers could drive cars.

To introduce AI successfully, subject matter experts need to be trained. They need the opportunity to practise using the technology, like getting a driver's licence. The goal is to avoid creating AI solutions from scratch in the same way that we don't need to manufacture cars from scratch to use them.

WHERE IS YOUR ORGANISATION TODAY?

Søren Kierkegaard said, "If you want to move a person from one place to another, you have to meet him where he is."[2] This principle also applies to organisations. To improve your AI adoption, you must first evaluate your current state and work out where your organisation is at. You can do so by referring to these four adoption states.

- curious
- opportunistic
- strategic
- ignorant

Discussing the current state of AI adoption can facilitate agreement on the path forward. Often, people aren't aligned and have different perceptions of where they stand. Agreeing on actions to improve the situation can be challenging without alignment. Therefore, starting by identifying your current state is helpful.

Curious

Companies that have no prior experience with AI and seek information to understand how it can benefit them are in a *curious* state. They often have high expectations of what AI can do for them but lack the knowledge to adopt it effectively.

These companies often have questions like:

- Where do we start?
- What do we need to know?
- How do we get inspiration?

Executives in these companies reach out to consultants and experts, saying, "We have AI on the agenda at our upcoming board meeting. We don't know what to tell them. Can you help us?"

There's usually some healthy hesitancy in AI-curious companies. They want to understand if AI is for them before they invest in it. If a company is interested in AI but lacks knowledge and experience, starting with learning and gaining inspiration is essential. This involves understanding the fundamental building blocks and exploring successful use cases.

If your company is curious about AI, you must determine which business results you want to enhance using the technology. Common mistakes people make at this stage include hiring data scientists or buying expensive data platforms before they've identified opportunities for its application.

Opportunistic

Opportunist organisations hastily choose a project and begin developing an AI solution, often driven by their management team. They tend to view AI as purely technical, leading them to hire data scientists and other technical staff before they understand what they want to achieve and why.

Some even acquire AI platforms they then try to massage to solve problems they haven't yet identified – an impossible task. For example, a company asked my advice on whether to purchase an expensive AI platform. I asked them about their specific plans for using that platform, but they had no concrete ideas. When companies are in an opportunistic state, AI implementation often doesn't result in improved business outcomes, leading to questions from management such as "Why are we investing in AI?" or "What value are we getting from AI?"

Companies in this state often have an AI project that failed to move past the prototype stage or didn't provide the expected business value.

Strategic

Who wants to be strategic and is prepared to admit they aren't?

A strategic approach to AI means you need to:

- Build a pipeline of project opportunities clearly stating the expected business value.
- Work with AI experts to estimate the effort required.
- Implement the solutions/opportunities that offer the best cost-benefit ratio.

You'll get a pipeline of different project opportunities. Some may be mundane, trivial, and inexpensive, while others will be strategic and expensive. That shouldn't come as a surprise. AI is a technology that can be used for various business challenges.

IGNORANT

Ignorant companies don't believe AI can solve their current issues or that it is a valuable technology. They may think it could be helpful in the future but don't believe it is at this stage yet.

The reality is that all companies already use AI in some form. They need to be shown how AI is already part of their work processes and how it could further improve them.

THREE ADOPTION STRATEGIES

There are three approaches for adopting AI in a company or organisation:

- Off-the-shelf AI
- Auto AI
- Custom AI

These approaches vary in technical knowledge and skill required to implement them. At the lower end of the scale is off-the-shelf AI, the easiest and least expensive option but also the least flexible. At the other end of the scale is custom AI. The latter demands a wide range of skills and often requires significant investment for development and maintenance, but it offers greater flexibility. Most people, by default, think of custom AI when considering using or adopting it. They overlook the opportunity to start off-the-shelf with less need for technical skills.

Understanding these differences isn't just relevant to technical personnel – it directly impacts your business. When choosing an AI strategy, you must consider your long-term willingness to invest in the necessary skills. Basing your approach on a single project won't be productive. Investing sporadically for one-off projects will lead to significant overheads. Additionally, there may be extended periods of overloaded data science and AI resources, followed by periods of underuse.

It may be beneficial to consider different strategies for in-house and out-house projects. For example, you could adopt off-the-shelf AI and autoAI solutions for in-house projects but rely on vendors and consultants for custom solutions. The critical step here is that you make a conscious choice.

The approach to AI adoption doesn't have to be a company-wide decision. For example, R&D departments in some companies may work with custom AI since they're constantly improving core products where even slight performance increases can make a significant difference. In contrast, off-the-shelf or autoAI solutions may be sufficient for departments such as automation, finance, or operations.

It's also not either/or. Many AI solutions are mixes of these strategies. For example, Paperflow was an AI company that adopted custom AI, but we still used OCR – an off-the-shelf solution.

Off-the-shelf AI

Off-the-shelf or ready-to-use AI products often come as software-as-a-service (SaaS) with a pay-per-use or subscription plan. Paperflow is such a service (from the customer's perspective). It is a high-touch SaaS, which means it has significant business impact and needs to be integrated into other software, such as enterprise resource planning or invoice management systems. Other off-the-shelf AI services, such as Google Translate, OCR, ChatGPT and speech-to-text, can be less intrusive.

You can also find off-the-shelf AI as modules in other software. Examples include your customer relationship management system, that can suggest which leads are the most promising, or the shift planner that can automatically allocate the best people for specific shifts.

Off-the-shelf AI has its limitations when it comes to customised solutions. What you see is what you get, and the solution is the same for everyone. For example, OCR can't be adjusted to the specific font in your documents. For this reason, off-the-shelf AIs are primarily used for generic problems like translation, recognising standard objects in images, or predicting general themes in texts.

This strategy for adopting AI requires little or no investment in technical skills. However, you may still need to integrate off-the-shelf AI with your other IT systems, which will require traditional software development.

AutoAI

AutoAI, also known as *autoML* or *automated machine learning*, works as a hybrid between off-the-shelf AI adoption and custom AI.

From a user perspective, it allows you to bring your unique data and build an AI model with little data science understanding. Often, AutoAI works by uploading data to a platform that automatically trains and hosts an AI model. Teachable Machine is an example. It allows you to upload images in separate folders and then trains a model ready for use.

AutoAI might not meet your needs as precisely as custom AI. You can't tweak the algorithm yourself, so some opportunities for improving performance will be lost. However, autoAI still provides flexibility in training models and using data, and its cost is relatively low. A model built with AutoAI can cost as little as $20 in consumption costs, and the time to build it can be as short as a few minutes. Most AutoAI solutions take a few hours, which is still less than the coding usually needed with custom AI. AutoAI is also readily available through major providers like Google and Microsoft, making it a straightforward option for companies already using cloud solutions.

You could also argue that LLMs provided by cloud providers are turning into AutoAI, as they can now be fine-tuned with your data, so they have domain-specific information or ways of writing.

AutoAI deployment and usage typically require minimal maintenance, as many providers offer hosting services. Using such providers, you can outsource staying current with the latest models and techniques in the field. That's one of the most significant benefits of AutoAI.

Some use AutoAI as a benchmark or prototype. If you want to build a solution with custom AI, you can start with AutoAI to see what accuracy level you should expect from a custom model. For example, if your autoML is 50% accurate, expecting a custom model to be 90% correct without better data would be unreasonable. However, if your AutoAI model is 80%, it might be possible for your custom model to achieve 90% accuracy.

There are a few potential drawbacks with AutoAI. One is that if you rely on it heavily and later decide you need more customisation, you may feel locked into your chosen provider. Sometimes, the only option may be to start over with a fully customised setup.

AutoAI also has limitations regarding its building blocks. Not all building blocks are available in this setup, and some vendors might offer only a few. Tabular data models still require that the user is experienced in working with data. Furthermore, it's uncommon to find providers that can build unsupervised learning models with AutoAI.

Custom AI

Custom AI means you develop the solutions with the help of machine learning engineers and data scientists and through frameworks such as Tensorflow or PyTorch.

This approach introduces a series of challenges that you need specialists for:

data analysis and modelling

machine learning operations for hosting and scaling models

software development for building glue code

The advantage of custom AI is that you can build what you want how you want it. You can use your own data and tune (adjust) the models while having better insight into how they work.

Custom AI usually has low running costs. The higher the number of queries to the model, the more economically beneficial it becomes.

SUMMARY

Adopting AI requires educating your organisation about the technology and its basics. This will enable your employees to identify opportunities quickly and with enthusiasm. AI adoption can't succeed from managerial directives alone. It's a bottom-up technology that requires domain experts to be involved. Before starting AI adoption initiatives, assess your organisation's current adoption level: is it curious, opportunistic, strategic, or ignorant? Agreeing with your colleagues on this assessment will avoid hiring technical people too early. Finally, choosing an AI adoption strategy should ensure that competencies and ambitions match.

CHAPTER 5
SOLVING PROBLEMS USING AI

AI presents distinct challenges and opportunities beyond what we encounter in other IT areas. The transition from instruction-based to example-based systems necessitates a paradigm shift that may appear counterproductive in other IT contexts. It makes it easy for novices to fall prey to the numerous pitfalls in this field. The high failure rate of 87% in AI projects is evidence of that.

Two distinct characteristics of AI make it essential to develop an implementation method. Uncertainty is the first. This demands a means of managing any lack of knowledge about the necessary data, the quantity required, and the expected performance of AI models. It's essential when the AI solution involves stakeholders unfamiliar with the technology, who might not understand how it alters your ability to construct a business case. The second is AI's abundant opportunities (which may seem counterintuitive). AI model outputs can be unpredictable and unforeseeable, especially with the latest advances in generative models like ChatGPT.

My method – the *Todai Method* – makes the process more manageable. It's structured chronologically to help you avoid setbacks caused by doing things in the wrong order.

When developing AI solutions, it's challenging to construct a business case or guarantee the model's performance. In fact, in the initial stages of the development process, there's no certainty that a solution can be created. Navigating stakeholder relationships in such an environment can be highly demanding. Managers, financial personnel, and even potential investors may struggle to comprehend why you can't outline the cost of the solution or how it will function before you develop it. Customers, users, and salespeople might have trouble understanding why you can't accurately predict the AI's performance. Some may argue that AI is ineffective and worthless if it isn't 100% precise.

The Todai Method lets you specify the stage at which you'll address stakeholders' questions. It also allows you to identify the point at which they can halt or diverge, providing a clear roadmap to minimise risks. This is especially beneficial when dealing with management since they will have confidence in the process and allow you to carry out the task without repeated intervention.

Additionally, the Todai Method lets you communicate with stake-holders without technical jargon. At the end of each phase, you can cut your losses or jump back to a previous one and make changes. Building a project plan is much easier when you know the phases and activities involved. Starting from blank paper or with no agenda other than "let's solve a problem with AI" is bound to fail.

METHODS AREN'T NEW

Frameworks that align IT and business (such as Design Thinking for solution design and SCRUM for agile development) are widely used. Still, however, the significance of a suitable framework with AI has yet to be noticed. This is especially the case when bridging business needs with technological possibilities. AI's explorative nature and classification as an innovative technology may have contributed to this oversight.

The data science field offers an extensive range of methods, many of which have existed for years. However, frameworks like CRISP-DM and KDNugget prioritise technical and data mining over discovering the solution's business impact. For example, while CRISP-DM acknowledges the activity of "identifying the users' needs and expectations," it presumes users are aware of what they want or need. The fundamental challenge in AI and data science is aligning the technology's potential with business opportunities in an environment where users may need a greater understanding of what is feasible.

THE TODAI METHOD

The Todai Method recognises that the primary challenge of AI resides in non-technical activities.

It works for all aspects of applying AI. The difference between building a forecasting model in fast-moving consumer goods and image recognition in agriculture is staggeringly small. The same goes for using an off-the-shelf approach to building custom AI solutions. Best practices, tools, and activities are generally the same regardless of the type of AI model.

The method is divided into phases, with activities, objectives, and best practices. It also highlights potential pitfalls.

METHOD STEPS

The method is comprised of six steps.

1. inspiration
2. discovery
3. data handling
4. development
5. implementation
6. monitoring

USING THE METHOD

Following the method will help you remember the small details that could lead to disaster if you ignore them. It provides a basis for planning and communicating with stakeholders before and during your project.

You can use this method for the activities in each phase. When you enter a new phase, it's worth reminding yourself of potential pitfalls.

The phases include a list of goals and activities you can use to decide whether you'll proceed to the next phase. It's essential to agree explicitly on how to measure these objectives. For example, in the discovery phase, designing a decision model could be an objective that must be achieved to proceed. Another example is the data phase, which involves measuring the cost of data. Here, you can agree on a maximum price for data. If the price exceeds this limit, continuing will be unfeasible.

When stakeholders feel uneasy about uncertainties associated with AI-based projects, you can reduce their anxiety by taking the initiative for the next step. A general guideline is that no more than twenty-four hours should elapse between completing a phase or activity and providing stakeholders with a detailed plan for the next phase or activity.

1. INSPIRATION PHASE

The inspiration phase is about finding critical opportunities for utilising AI and evaluating their viability. It starts with identifying a business outcome and is often initiated when someone says, "We want to apply AI, but we don't know how to get started."

A lack of ideas about how AI can help achieve the desired business outcomes can be the most significant barrier to getting started. Most people understand that AI has enormous potential but have trouble connecting this to their business and pointing out exactly where it can provide value. That's what you deal with in the inspiration phase.

You also address feasibility testing via a pre-analysis that assesses the business readiness and technical viability of applying AI to one or more potential opportunities.

2. DISCOVERY

During the discovery phase, your primary objectives are to:

1. Develop a comprehensive understanding of the problem you must resolve.
2. Establish a design incorporating both the AI solution and the associated business processes.

That includes connecting the problem and suggested solutions to the company strategy. A common problem is that many AI initiatives are born as *satellite projects*. In other words, they have no connection to the overall strategy or a specific outcome. The discovery phase will help you avoid satellite status.

When you acquire domain knowledge and involve domain experts during this phase, you can solve the problem more efficiently. It also means less resistance later. A facet of this phase is to be aware of the accuracy requirements of the models so you're clear about what's "good enough."

The second part of the discovery phase emphasises solution design. Here, decision-making plays a significant role. The primary consideration is how to transform the model output into practical decisions. This process, known as *decision modelling*, is crucial to the discovery phase.

Developing a decision model can be challenging as it typically involves numerous individuals and departments. People often postpone this task, only to realise later that it alters solution requirements or halts the project's progress due to an inability to reach an agreement.

The discovery phase typically presents the most significant challenges when implementing AI. At some point, the issues previously mentioned surface, and the consequences can be costly. For example, with Paperflow, we needed an extensive understanding of domain knowledge, which took us over a year of development and was very expensive.

3. DATA HANDLING

The data phase covers the acquisition, preparation, and analysis of the data that will be used for training AI models. As you begin working with data, you'll gain new insights into the problem space. Sometimes, you can validate insights from the discovery phase. At other times, the data will contradict what the domain experts claimed. These insights can be precious.

Labelling can be a central activity when it comes to data in AI. This process can be costly and time-consuming and, as a result, significantly impacts the business case. In Paperflow, we had to label millions of invoices and mark the total amount, date, and invoice lines. We could calculate the cost of labelling each invoice. Imagine that the price was $1 versus **10c per invoice**. With millions of invoices, this translates into a lot of money and can make or break the business case.

4. DEVELOPMENT

In this phase, you train and develop the models. When building your models, you'll gain insight into their accuracy and the results you get. That's critical in AI, especially considering that you'll also have to convey this information to other project stakeholders who haven't spent the same amount of time as you working through the ins and outs of the technology.

During this phase, you also conduct actual result testing with users. If you do this correctly, you'll gain their trust and receive feedback that will steer you in the right direction.

At this point, you build retraining flows to keep the models improving or at least staying as accurate as possible.

5. IMPLEMENTATION

Now the AI solution is ready, you'll implement and deploy it into other IT systems to make it live and available. At this point, users are supposed to adopt and love it. That means you did an adequate job in the discovery phase and built a solution your users need.

Even if all is perfect, you can still meet resistance. Some people need help to accept the conditions of working with AI solutions. For example, the likely output is contrary to other IT solutions where you know what you'll get when you click a button. Also, some outputs might seem incorrect when people don't understand how models arrive at their results.

The ideal scenario is that the users love the AI solution and are happy to adopt it. This is likely if you've built the solution they need.

6. MONITORING

Even when you've implemented the AI solution, and users have adopted it, the task is still ongoing.

A common misunderstanding is that AI models learn and improve as they see more data in production. The media's narrative makes it sound like an AI solution – say, a self-driving car – performs better the more it drives. The opposite is true. As a default, performance deteriorates over time.

Models are trained on data collected at a specific point in time. Unless you make an active effort to update them, their accuracy will gradually diminish. For example, new road sign designs could become more challenging for AI to recognise since they weren't part of its training data. Similarly, people could suddenly start riding electric scooters, generating new, unanticipated data in the wild that might cause the model to perform poorly.

This concept of AI becoming less accurate is called *drifting*. The model drifts away from the real world as it changes over time. Luckily, there are ways of measuring this drift and alerting you when it's too high. You'll have to retrain the model with new data when that happens.

MILESTONE FUNDING

Milestone funding involves releasing funds for the next phase only if you've met the goals of the previous one. Combining the Todai Method with milestone funding lets you control the cost.

The goals can be anything from achieving positive user tests, model accuracy, or acquiring a certain amount of data within a budget. For example, it might turn out that your data is insufficient or of poor quality. Resolving that issue requires more funding. It's possible to negotiate a release of additional funding if your goals aren't satisfied, but that becomes a conscious and transparent decision. In this negotiation, you can reconsider the scope of the solution. A smaller scope is worth considering if the costs are higher than acceptable.

Milestone funding allows you to gather additional information about the solution as you progress. Each new piece of data enables you to decide whether to provide more funding or halt the project at each milestone. It can seem like too much overhead having to agree on funding several times, but it allows you to adjust your scope or cut losses early.

If your organisation isn't accustomed to milestone funding, you might feel uneasy about the possibility of halting the project midway. However, over time, this approach can result in fewer expensive failures and increased trust from the people involved in applying AI.

MIND THE MINDSET

The stakeholders' mindset is fundamental to the success of implementing AI. You need to allow for different perspectives when building AI solutions. Each mood presents unique challenges in the AI development process.

Most employees have an operational mindset. That also goes for most project stakeholders, especially domain experts. People have a job to do. When you bring in new technology, of which they don't know the implications, you are the disturber of the peace. They might be intrigued by AI but think they don't have time to fool around with new technology. Deadlines are approaching, and everyone is busy.

Few people excel in all the different mindsets. Typically, individuals have a comfort zone in one mindset and can adapt to others to some extent. However, transitioning from a creative mindset to an operational one is a challenging skill that only some master.

There are a few tricks that make it easier to work with the participants' mindsets:

Be vocal

Tell the stakeholders what mindset they should have for each phase. That way, you can diffuse frustration among stakeholders unfamiliar with the currently required perspective.

Take people to new physical venues

If you take the participants outside their natural habitat, they become more open and focused on the task, as their everyday work is out of sight and out of mind.

Let other people take charge when you aren't the right person

If you don't have the mindset for a specific part of the project, it's best to delegate the responsibility. Too many projects fail as operational people discount everything new in the early stages. Just as many fail from creative people thinking the job is done when a model can make a prediction. Before a project starts, identify the people with the appropriate mindset to handle each phase.

BUILDING AI IS LIKE DEVELOPING A PRODUCT

When building AI solutions, don't consider the process as you would for a project. Instead, think of it as if you're building a product. When building products, the process is distinct in that they're centred around the final users. The main goal is to get them to adopt and love the product. That means other stakeholders, even the business sponsors, have a lower priority. You need the same perspective for every AI solution – they all have users, and their success is directly related to the solution's success.

That product-building methods work well in AI isn't a coincidence. AI solutions are more like products than one-off projects. The tools and techniques that improve success with AI are often taken from product-building practices. Despite this, AI solutions are usually built with a *project* mentality. Projects and products differ in their core goals and characteristics. The core objective of projects is delivery by specifications on time and within an agreed budget. You decide on the deliveries with the project's key stakeholders, and when you check the boxes, it's considered delivered. In a product, the goal is to continuously solve a core problem for the users that you can measure through user feedback and user adoption.

The core characteristics of a project are:

- Alternative solutions are examined via a business case.
- Agreed on concrete objectives to be delivered before the project is initiated. On their completion, the project will be considered closed.
- Projects are monitored through deadlines of deliveries and sub-deliveries.
- Users and their interaction and satisfaction with the solution are the core measurements.
- Alternatives are examined via users' alternative products or solutions to their problems.
- Roadmaps and constant improvements are the default. When the product is built, and the first users are onboarded, you're only at the beginning of the journey.

AI solutions are dynamic as they rely on data. As this data is expected to reflect the world in which it operates, and that includes user behaviour, it will inevitably change over time. As the data changes, so does the accuracy of predictions, business outcomes, and user experiences. Consequently, you need to anticipate changes in how the solution is used, its correlation to business outcomes, and the allocation of resources for modifying updates to the scope.

HOW TO BE PRODUCT-FOCUSED

To be product-focused, you must make the users your centre of measuring success – not prediction accuracy, data quality, or state-of-the-art algorithms. The main goals are user adoption, satisfaction, and user value.

In the early phases of building your AI solution, you must identify when you've satisfied the user's needs. Once the solution is live, those needs are a continuous measure of success.

Imagine you're building an AI solution to categorise documents for an administrative task in a company. The measure of success shouldn't be how correct the categorisation is, but how users consider the solution helps them perform their job.

It can be helpful to find out which methods users currently employ for the task (for example, a keyword search) so you can compare their results with those offered by AI. Doing it manually might turn out to be a more efficient approach.

MEASURE USER ADOPTION AND MAKE IT YOUR RESPONSIBILITY

If the users don't use the solution, it's not because they dislike change or are ignorant. You've probably made a mistake or have failed to communicate and convince them of the value.

If you put user adoption as a part of your business case, this responsibility becomes very clear. Suppose you have 200 people performing a task that you're building an AI solution to support. It could be a classic churn prediction model that tells the sales team which customers might cancel their contracts soon. Most people who build business cases do so, assuming everyone will start using the solution almost *immediately* and *correctly*. Adding those parameters to your business case can turn a no-brainer case into a loss.

See this equation:

Expected value from solution * percentage of users adopting * how well the users use the software.

If the value of the churn prediction solution was €500,000, but only 30% adopt and use AI somewhat correctly (say, 50% utilisation), you have this value:

500.000 * 0.3 * 0. 5 = € 75,000

That's only 15% of the original value left. You get what you measure, and as adoption is crucial to the business case, you must assess it.

THINK LIKE A PRODUCT MANAGER

A *product* manager has commercial and technical responsibilities. Their job is to facilitate user needs through the capabilities of developers, data scientists, user experience (UX) designers, and data engineers to maximise the product's value over its lifetime. It isn't to take a pre-defined set of requirements and ask others to implement them – that's the role of a *project* manager. In other words, the role of a project manager is to read the IKEA manual for building a cupboard and guide the project members to assemble it effectively and correctly. On the other hand, the product manager's task is to identify the storage solution that addresses the user's need, which may involve suggesting a cupboard as a solution.

BUILD A PRODUCT VISION

A product must have a vision that employees should constantly support evangelically. Whether you're building a product for internal or external use, the critical task is making potential users and stakeholders buy into the vision. Solutions for internal purposes tend to be dictated to users, as they're employees with no choice but to say yes. Think of the users as external customers who should be delighted to buy and adopt the product.

FIND PRODUCT MARKET FIT

When building products, the most demanding challenge is to make the product fit the market. Who are the users? What do users need? What are their alternatives to the solution you are building? You should ask yourself the same questions while building solutions using AI.

USER EXPERIENCE DESIGN

Don't underestimate the need for user experience design (UX) when building AI solutions with user interaction. UX is often more important than the AI model and its accuracy to achieve a successful outcome.

Including a UX designer early in the process will ensure usability. Creating wireframes or prototype designs and conducting user testing before training the model can help ensure a good user experience. Additionally, UX tests can reveal the information users need from the model and what they expect to see in the output displayed in a user interface. This can make the solution more tangible in the early stages of development.

The bottom line is that projects have stakeholders, and products have users. As AI needs users, it needs a product-focused approach. This principle is an integral part of the method.

SUMMARY

Getting started with your first AI-based solution will be different from the IT solutions you might be used to undertaking – the level of uncertainty is high. High uncertainty calls for a different approach. If you follow the phases, their objectives and best practices I recommend, you will increase your chances of success, especially if you combine this with milestone funding.

I also recommend treating AI like building products. You need to please your users, not managers or other stakeholders. Without user adoption, the solution is worthless.

CHAPTER 6
INSPIRATION PHASE

If you have already settled on what business opportunity or specific problem you're trying to solve and know its feasibility, then you can skip the inspiration phase. This is often the case when the opportunity is an offspring of another related application of AI.

However, if you are looking for areas where AI could be beneficial, you should start with an inspiration phase.

First, you decide on a business outcome. That could be trying to win more sales orders in a production company, planning resources better in a hospitality business, or improving animal welfare on a farm. You're trying to identify opportunities where AI solutions can support the company's strategy.

OBJECTIVES

- identifying one or more opportunities for applying AI towards a specific outcome
- testing technical feasibility and business viability of using AI to exploit these opportunities
- building business cases

ACTIVITIES

- upskilling domain experts
- brainstorming for ideas
- conducting a pre-analysis

The inspiration phase may appear to focus on identifying areas to implement AI simply to utilise the technology, reminiscent of the saying, "when you have a hammer, everything looks like a nail." It might feel forced, but that's unlikely to be an issue as long as you embrace feasibility testing that includes the potential outcome of "not feasible." Over time, as participants become more familiar with AI, they can recognise opportunities for its application. Most businesses possess numerous potential AI use cases. The challenge lies in refraining from initiating too many AI projects simultaneously and prematurely.

Sometimes, the inspiration phase doesn't identify any worthwhile opportunities. That's fine. It may not always be the right time or situation to incorporate AI. If your business isn't prepared to allocate time to learn about AI and explore its intricacies, it's better to delay adopting it. However, AI is becoming increasingly affordable and accessible; eventually, all businesses will embrace it.

It can take a long time, even a year, from inspiration to discovery. This phase might even spark a business strategy review. This could involve deciding on the adoption strategies from the previous chapter. Or newly obtained knowledge about AI could reveal new business opportunities.

The inspiration phase needs a creative, explorative, and open mindset. It's about exploring opportunities. It's human nature to jump to solutions, but if you lock-in too early, you could miss out on far better opportunities. Another problem with too much solution eagerness is that people talk about why a specific solution isn't viable and the whole problem is suddenly deemed "not viable for AI."

Keeping an open mind and not looking for a specific idea or solution too early is essential.

TRAINING PEOPLE TO IDENTIFY OPPORTUNITIES

Working with AI often involves venturing into domains where you might not possess expertise, even when developing internal solutions for your organisation. By training subject matter experts, you get ideal individuals to pinpoint opportunities or problems you can address using AI. The alternative is for AI specialists to acquire sufficient domain knowledge to recognise the right opportunities, but that is too time-consuming.

The primary limitation for domain experts, as the key opportunity detectives, is their unfamiliarity with AI. With basic training, you can overcome this limitation and enable them to generate numerous poten-tially valuable ideas. When training domain experts, you must include the following elements:

AI definition: Establish a clear definition of AI to ensure participants share the same understanding. (You can refer to the definition provided in Chapter 2.) It's essential to address the uncertainty inherent in AI, as understanding this concept can be challenging, espe-cially for domain experts who take pride in accurate and error-free work.

Building blocks: The experts can use the building blocks to match their ideas with AI functionality. Show industry-relevant examples for each building block.

Make them build AI: Nothing beats learning by doing. Include tools such as Teachable Machine or ChatGPT. It makes more sense once the domain experts have seen the process from data to model to prediction.

MAKE AI ACCESSIBLE

When instructing others about AI, aim to make the content as practical and approachable as possible. A common error when teaching AI is to emphasise its complexity. Instead, focus on its practical applications. There's no need to showcase diagrams of neural networks, mention specific algorithms, or dive into the complexities of machine learning. People have a limited capacity for absorbing new concepts, so ensure that everything taught is applicable and essential for identifying opportunities. Otherwise, you risk participants retaining unnecessary information while overlooking more important matters.

IDEA WORKSHOP

The idea workshop is a brainstorming session on generating ideas for applying AI. Before the workshop, it's beneficial to conduct interviews with participants so you can better understand their specific contexts.

A *pre-interview* is a screening conversation that takes place before the full interview. It eases participants into the process and piques their curiosity by giving them a glimpse of what's to come. They'll be eager to see how their insights are used. This makes them more engaged during the workshop, attentive, and will likely contribute to more valuable ideas.

Ideally, you should hold at least two thirty-minute interviews with each participant. It can be useful to select contrasting individuals based on their skills or job roles – one technical and the other as non-technical as possible.

Questions could include:

- What does the term "AI" mean to you?
- What worries you most about the idea of working with AI?
- How do you think AI could help you in your role?
- In what ways do you think AI could be part of your job in the future?
- What do you hope to gain from this workshop?

Answers to these questions provide the necessary insights into the participants' current (and often very different) understanding of AI. It also shows how fixed they are on specific solutions that might need untangling at the workshop. If they already have ideas about applying AI, you can use these as examples to explain the building blocks. That makes the training more relevant and engages the participants. Their understanding will skyrocket.

ADD A PRETOTYPE

If time permits, consider incorporating a presentation of a pretotype[1] model.

To achieve this, request that some participants provide data before the workshop for model-building purposes. The data doesn't need to be tailored to solve any particular problem. Use an AutoAI tool to create a model using the provided data, which should take no more than two or three hours.

During the session, present the data used, explain the model training process, and demonstrate its performance using new data. Familiar data will enable participants to engage more easily and better comprehend AI.

If obtaining participant data isn't feasible, you could explore industry-relevant datasets on Kaggle.com. Demonstrating that AI models are accessible and achievable makes it easier for participants to envision developing AI-based solutions.

DESIGN SPRINTS

A *design sprint* is a five-day process – a working week – that takes you quickly through idea generation, testing small prototypes and learning if they work. You'll need to do some preparation, including making sure the people you need are available.

If you follow the process outlined below, you can avoid getting caught up in debate and get things moving fast. Once you've gathered enough information, you can work with a prototype instead of waiting until you're ready to launch the final version.

For example:

Day 1: *Define the problem and work out where you will focus.* The first day is about having structured conversations to build a foundation for the rest of the sprint. You'll need to define key questions and your long-term goal. When you've worked out a simple map of your product or service, you can ask everyone on your team to share their knowledge. That will help you determine what approach offers the best opportunities and where the most significant risks might lie.

Day 2: *Start sketching out possible solutions on paper.* Rather than brainstorming, everyone involved will work on their solution in detail.

Day 3: *Decide which of your ideas is strongest.* After Day 2, you'll probably have several solutions you can choose from. Rather than getting entangled in endless debate or making a compromise decision, no one is pleased with; once everyone has shared their idea, ask them to vote on their favourite solution. It's best if they do this simultaneously, so no one can influence anyone else.

Day 4: *Build a realistic prototype.* Your prototype will simulate a finished product for your customers. It may not be perfect, but it will get you on the right track.

Day 5: *Test your prototype on human users.* Show your prototype to five users in five separate one-on-one interviews. Get as much feedback as you can. This method will help you to get answers to your most pressing questions right away.

PRE-ANALYSIS

Conducting a pre-analysis is useful in reducing uncertainty. It can also offer insight into the potential costs and value of the proposed solution.

The objectives of a pre-analysis should include:

- gaining an understanding of the problem and desired outcome

- acquiring domain knowledge
- identifying the required data and assessing its accessibility
- obtaining an initial insight into the expected model accuracy
- evaluating if the proposed solution meets the business needs

You can incorporate concepts from the other phases of this method to accomplish these objectives, making the pre-analysis a condensed version of the entire project. This approach allows you to select and apply tools and activities as you see fit. Here are some activities I typically include.

DECISION MODELS

Decision modelling, which I will go into in more detail later, can assist you in mapping how AI predictions translate into actions and decisions.

The decision model exercise also reveals the preparedness of project stakeholders to integrate models into their business processes. If you detect misalignment while creating the decision model, address it before proceeding. You may also find that stakeholders aren't prepared to implement the necessary business process changes to apply the solution. AI models become ineffective if their predictions can't be converted into actions.

The decision model needs to be specific regarding the actions it describes and cover all model outcomes. For example, it should exclude actions such as "then the user decides what to do." This makes it more reliable in terms of business needs. Decisions must contribute to the desired business outcome you're targeting.

ASK FOR DATA

Ask for data access in the pre-analysis. By doing this, you'll be able to work out the costs associated with acquiring and preparing the data you need. Sometimes you will experience getting access within a few hours and at others up to a year. If you must wait six months for data, that's six months of the project on hold. The sooner you can identify data acquisition challenges, the better.

Accessing data can be difficult due to technical as well as organisational or legal barriers. In the EU, the data can be subject to the General Data Protection Regulation (GDPR), requiring a decent amount of paperwork. With AI being relatively new, many legal departments are unsure how to handle this.

Once you can access the data, you can develop an understanding of your problem and any potential issues that might arise. For example, you may need to consider:

- How many different labels are there?
- How many examples per label?
- How often is the data updated?
- Does the data seem reliable?

Businesses tend to be either overly optimistic or excessively sceptical about their data. For example, I once worked on an image classification solution with a company that thought they had vast amounts of data. But when the data came, the class of images we wanted to identify only had one example among thousands. Early access to data will uncover challenges and help you understand the cost side of the business case.

BUILD MODELS

As soon as data becomes available, build a few pretotype models. For example, if you want to identify mould in a food processing factory, you can create an image classification model using images from the production line.

The objective is to obtain an initial indication of the potential model accuracy. If the model can correctly identify mould in the factory 95% of the time, it offers a hint of the value that could be derived from the solution. This information helps you create a concrete and data-driven business case.

Another benefit of creating a model is the discovery of numerous aha! moments. You might discover that the results from food plants are so different that you need separate images from each plant. Or you might need to make environmental adjustments to the camera to improve the model's performance in new factories.

This process also helps determine if you're using the correct data. For example, in a housing price predictor, you might discover that the feature "does the house have a garage?" has no significant impact on the prediction output. Although this observation may not be definitive, it's a valuable point to discuss with domain experts during the discovery phase.

INTERVIEW DOMAIN EXPERTS

As part of the pre-analysis, you must interview domain experts. While you'll also do this during the discovery phase, the interviews in the inspiration phase will be more exploratory. The inspiration phase interviews concentrate on questions about the business outcome rather than the solution. Both domain experts and AI designers tend to jump to solution-based thinking too quickly, so be cautious.

LOOK WHAT OTHERS HAVE DONE

In pre-analysis, you need to research and get inspiration from what others have done. Google or Bing are your friends, and you'd be surprised how many problems have already been solved with AI.

When I first encountered the problem of "detecting pneumonia in pigs by their cough," I thought it was a rare case with little precedence. A quick internet search told me that many companies had dealt with it, and many research articles had been published on the subject. This research will give you a head start and save you from potentially reinventing the wheel.

INSPIRATION PHASE CHECKLIST

To transition to the discovery phase, you can use the following checklist:

- Everyone involved has gained a basic understanding of AI's building blocks.
- You've consulted domain experts.
- The data you need is available or has been requested.
- Research on AI in this specific domain has been conducted.
- A particular problem or opportunity has been identified based on the above. (This doesn't have to be a solution, and the scope may still change during the discovery phase.)

BUILDING THE BUSINESS CASE

Most businesses require the preparation of business cases for their decision-making processes, particularly for funding and resource allocation for new initiatives. This is a sensible approach, but creating a business case for AI can be challenging due to the technology's inherent uncertainties, explorative nature, and unpredictability.

The traditional business case approach isn't suitable for AI.

Ultimately, a business case is simply a tool used to make informed investment decisions. For AI, the goal is to incrementally collect information on costs and values to make well-informed decisions rather than adhering strictly to a traditional format that expects you to have it all up-front. Several factors can affect the AI solution's business case.

The problem-understanding. Understanding and scoping the problem is one of the most time-consuming aspects of an AI solution. Sometimes, the solution only becomes apparent once you fully understand the domain. This contrasts with traditional IT projects, which typically require most work during the coding and development phase.

Data and labelling. Since you don't know what data (features or data sources) you need or how much is required to achieve the desired accuracy, it's difficult to estimate the cost of data.

The complexity of labelling varies significantly between image classification, object recognition, and image segmentation. Each type is ten times more demanding than the previous one. A similar disparity exists between text classification and named entity recognition. At this point, you don't know what building blocks you'll be using. Hence, the data labelling cost is unpredictable.

Maintenance costs. Some models may experience drift, meaning you'll need to acquire new data and retrain the model continuously. However, you can't always predict the extent of drift or the requirements for retraining. Additionally, there can be associated costs for computer capacity running the retraining.

At this stage, you don't know if you can solve the problem using pre-trained off-the-shelf models, AutoAI, or custom models, which can significantly impact maintenance costs.

Much of the value of the AI solution comes from the following:

Model accuracy. Suppose your AI model can automatically predict to which department an email should be directed. This will reduce administrative costs and expedite customer service, leading to happier customers and maybe increased sales. Estimating the cost savings for a solution like this depends on the level of automation, which is tied to the accuracy you can achieve. The challenge is that minor differences in accuracy can have a significant impact. For example, the difference between 95% and 90% accuracy in redirecting emails might seem small, but it results in twice the amount of manual labour required for the lower accuracy. Since you can't determine a model's accuracy during the inspiration phase or when building the business case, it's impossible to predict this value before the discovery phase accurately.

The AI solution adoption. Adopting the AI solution also plays a significant role in determining its value. Many business cases tend to overestimate the ease with which users will adopt a new solution.

Building confidence in changes and new technology takes time and often significant effort.

MOVING FORWARD

The conventional approach to constructing business cases concentrates on the "what" aspects, such as the problem, costs, and required resources to develop the solution. This approach might not be suitable for AI.

The business case for AI should describe "how" it can be built. You can ask key questions such as, "How do we pinpoint the right problem to solve?" and "How do we identify the data we need?" This will enable you to create a list of activities to estimate expenses and better understand the AI solution's actual costs over time.

Your AI's business case is always a work in progress and should be updated at the end of each phase.

SET GOALS AND CALCULATE BACKWARDS

It's impossible to predict the model's accuracy when estimating an AI solution's potential value. To address this uncertainty, set accuracy goals for the model and create three versions of your business case based on different accuracy levels. For example, if you aim for an 85% accurate document classification model, you can also calculate the business case for 80% and 90% accuracy. While this approach isn't perfect, the range of estimates brings you closer to making an informed decision.

ASSUME EVERYTHING WILL GO WRONG

A traditional business case template features a "what can go wrong and how can we avoid it" section. However, given the high level of uncertainty in AI projects, it's best to anticipate everything going wrong and plan accordingly.

Chances are you'll need to alter the project's scope and direction at least once. Therefore, it's helpful to develop a strategy for negotiating changes and determine who the decision-makers for pivots will be.

If you anticipate that the AI may make significant errors in production, you'll be better able to prepare for those situations. It's best to allocate time to create processes or IT solutions to manage such failures.

Similarly, you must ensure that users are trained to understand what to expect and how to handle potential issues. Building confidence in the AI solution may be challenging, and users may require time to adapt to and comprehend its capabilities.

SECURE STAKEHOLDER SUPPORT

It's crucial to secure stakeholder buy-in. They must understand that the traditional business case approach may not apply to AI projects. Convincing stakeholders in a conventional business setting may be tricky, but leveraging milestone funding can help change the business case approach. It also simplifies cutting losses if the situation deteriorates when more information is acquired.

Generative AI makes the business case even less tangible

Generative AI doesn't have an accuracy percentage on which you can base backwards calculations like predictive AI has. For example, the output of ChatGPT that writes an automated answer to a support email could read, "Dear customer, please provide your order number." This can't be said to be correct or incorrect, and you can't measure how correct it is automatically.

The output doesn't come with a confidence score, so you can't (currently) automate in the same way with a decision model, saying that if you're more than 95% sure the answer is correct, you can automate the process and accept 5% mistakes. You need to know you're above a certain confidence level to automate a decision (such as automatically sending a support reply to a customer). Output is subjectively understood and affects several "human" parameters. For example, an automated support email isn't just a matter of how much faster the email is written (average answer time minus generation time plus validation time). It's also a question of how much better or worse the answer is. If an AI written email is better or worse, it impacts customer satisfaction, which can also affect its value.

As a result, it's even harder to estimate the value of generative AI. This leads to the output value not being able to be measured before development. This is where a prototype in a pre-analysis stage is required.

SUMMARY

After completing the inspiration phase, you'll probably have identified one or more realistic AI implementation opportunities. You should also have an idea of the potential accuracy, gained some domain knowledge, and acquired insight into areas to investigate further as you transition into the discovery phase.

CHAPTER 7

DISCOVERY –
UNDERSTANDING THE
PROBLEM

Understanding the problem is half the solution.

No doubt you've heard this statement before. It's why your doctor won't start treatment before a diagnosis has been made.

The objective of the discovery phase is to thoroughly understand the problem before you devise a solution. Exploring and examining the problem is essential when working with AI, yet it's frequently overlooked.

In general, applying AI to solve critical business issues is no different to investing in anything else that requires effort, costs money or is associated with risk. You must explain why you want to do it and justify the required effort.

There are good reasons for rephrasing this fundamental step in generic problem-solving.

The first reason is that many AI solutions lack an apparent problem to solve. It's not that a problem isn't chosen. The challenge is that the understanding of the problem is inadequate, and the definition too weak. Achieving an in-depth problem definition is a significant part of the discipline of AI. And it's a skill any practitioner in this field needs to develop.

The second reason is that there's no alignment. Stakeholders will think they're working on the same problem and solution while having vastly different perceptions. This is common in numerous fields and disciplines, but AI is particularly affected due to its intangibility.

Not having a clear definition and alignment means unrealised business value and an overspent budget. These issues are often not visible before the later phases of building the solution – possibly not until the production stage.

In addition, if perceptions aren't aligned, chances are that even the best possible solution will only satisfy a fraction of your stakeholders.

DISCOVERY PHASE

The discovery phase is as explorative as the inspiration phase. The difference is that you no longer explore possible problems to solve or opportunities to pursue – they've already been identified. Instead, you work to understand and define each problem in depth and outline a solution. It's common to settle on a solution and post-rationalise reasons why it's optimal. Dividing this phase into two parts helps you avoid this mistake.

1. define and understand the problem
2. define a solution

In this chapter, we're concerned with understanding the problem before settling on a specific solution. We'll look at the second part in the next chapter.

Presenting a solution may raise concerns about committing prematurely during the discovery phase. While it might resemble the traditional waterfall model, where planning precedes execution, outlining a solution in the discovery phase doesn't preclude updates in the solution design.

The discovery phase is an active form of planning. You can refine your solution design by gaining more information about the data and accumulating modelling results. However, a clear initial solution is crucial for productivity when transitioning to the data and development stages.

DISCOVERY PHASE ACTIVITIES

The activities of the first part of the discovery phase are:

- define a problem scope
- understand the problem domain
- align the project team on the definition of the problem
- acquire domain knowledge through subject matter experts

SOLVING THE RIGHT PROBLEM

WHAT ARE YOU TRYING TO ACHIEVE?

The uncertainty inherent in AI solutions can make it difficult to link the solution to the desired outcome. Even slight variations in problem scope may necessitate vastly different solutions due to it being based on examples and predictions. Two techniques can assist you in determining precise objectives for the project: embracing the feeling of being lost and frequently saying no.

The goal is to feel lost

I mistakenly settled on a problem definition too early in Paperflow and repeatedly see others doing the same. The initial goal should be verifying whether the problem definition is sufficiently accurate. When you begin working on an undertaking requiring the application of AI, you might believe you have a clear understanding of your objective. However, it takes some exploration to grasp the problem's many facets. It's normal for team members in an AI project to sometimes feel lost and this doesn't necessarily mean anything is going wrong.

The *Dunning-Kruger effect* says that when you possess limited knowledge of a field or task, you tend to overestimate your abilities significantly. As you gain more knowledge, you may start to underestimate your skills. That's why, at the beginning of a project, you may feel confident that you fully comprehend your objectives and might opt for a brief discovery phase. Feeling lost during the discovery phase is a positive sign, if not a necessity. If you're overconfident, you're likely still in the early stage of blissful unawareness. Feeling lost indicates you've begun understanding the problem's limitations, variations, and complexities.

Say no a lot

Saying the word *no* more than usual is one of the most effective strategies for settling an AI-related problem scope.

The primary objective of the early discovery stage is to embrace the chaos and focus on a specific problem and solution scope. When you feel lost, you need to narrow your scope and reduce the number of complications and variations you must manage.

Be ready to say "no" if stakeholders want to adapt your solution to multiple use cases, incorporating additional features and targeting several business outcomes simultaneously.

While connecting to an outcome is vital, it's essential to concentrate on one outcome at a time.

SELECTING A BUSINESS OUTCOME

An outcome is a measurable result at a strategic level. Examples include revenue growth, increased clientele, or reduced costs. The outcome must have direct value and meet two criteria:

- it must initiate specific actions
- it must produce a tangible monetary result

The monetary aspect is essential, as it requires identifying the value source. Even if your AI solution's outcome is "happier employees," you must determine if the value lies in cost savings on talent attraction, longer employee retention, or something else.

Assigning a monetary value to everything doesn't imply that the motivation behind building the solution is solely financial. It's simply a way of measuring your solution's success, which must be decided during the discovery phase. Determining how to measure success after a solution is built can only lead to post-rationalisation (in other words, it will be claimed a victory no matter what). It also makes the development process confusing as the goal is unclear making it hard to know if the team is working in the same direction.

A solution can be technical in nature, a process, or even a physical construction. For example, it could be a novel approach to managing customer support cases, such as an IT program that stores data on support cases.

Here's an example of an outcome and solution:

Outcome: Reduce waste from overproduction by 20%, while still fulfilling all orders in a factory that sometimes produces too little or too much of the product.

Solution: A forecasting model that predicts incoming orders, allowing for production adjustments.

With a clear distinction between outcomes and solutions, the next step is to select the outcome that best aligns with the overall strategy.

Let's examine two cases to explain the tools and methods used to explore a problem when building a solution with AI.

THE PAPERFLOW PROBLEM

In Paperflow, we immediately addressed the technical challenge of automatically extracting data from invoices. Unbeknown to us, we'd prematurely committed to a solution without thoroughly exploring the problem space. We believed our solution would save time and money, allowing book-keepers to allocate their work hours to more meaningful tasks than simply inputting invoices. However, invoice processing requires more than just data entry. Having already developed a solution before testing it with users, we had to find a way to make it fit. Had we understood our problem space first, I'm sure that wouldn't have happened.

THE SUNDAI PROBLEM

SundAI is a chain of twenty small ice cream shops in a temperate climate, meaning hot summers, cold winters, and unpredictable weather, making sales fluctuate wildly. It produces its own ice cream and external vendors provide waffles and toppings. Like many other small shops, its employees tend to be young with little prior work experience and work part-time.

SundAI's management decided that AI might help them predict more precisely how much ice cream each store would sell in a given time frame. They hadn't decided if that time frame should be days, hours, or minutes – typical for an early scope. So far, they've used financial data from their ERP system to extrapolate last year's performance.

But maybe there's a better way.

A forecasting solution requires a clearly defined problem. What exactly is the forecasting intended to resolve?

It may appear as though the outcome is already established; management has decided to implement AI-based forecasting to "help better forecast ice cream sales." However, this outcome isn't adequate. The problem lies in the absence of a direct connection to a single, valuable outcome.

There are potentially three distinct outcomes:

1. The finance department can accurately predict monthly revenue.
2. The store manager can determine the appropriate number of employees needed per shift
3. The optimal amount of ice cream can be ordered for each store

All these outcomes are use cases for a forecasting solution. Why not build a forecasting solution and achieve these desired outcomes simultaneously? Because each outcome may have unique solution requirements.

For financial forecasting, the primary objective is to estimate cumulative sales accurately. Since financial forecasting only necessitates monthly sales predictions, it would be acceptable if sales spiked over a weekend because of (for example) a local sporting event or better-than-expected weather. As a result, we might not require data sources such as weather forecasts and information on local events.

Additionally, we have a limited number of users with extensive forecasting expertise, determining how we can leverage domain knowledge. The domain experts will probably also be the solution's users. This potentially allows us to involve users in the discovery phase and simplify the adoption process.

Furthermore, we don't need to perform forecasting frequently. This implies a reduced need for automating predictions and data collection.

For store managers handling shift planning, the situation is significantly different. The forecasting must account for fluctuations due to local events and incorporate weather data. Otherwise, we risk overstaffing on a rainy day with few customers or understaffing on a busy day when a popular soccer match occurs nearby.

Simultaneously, we must consider the notice period required for staff scheduling. If employees need a fourteen-day warning, it could pose a challenge, as weather forecasts become less reliable when looking more than a week ahead. This wouldn't be an issue for the financial use case.

If shift planning is the intended outcome, we also need to be capable of forecasting at an hourly level, as demand peaks may be brief, and it's unnecessary to maintain a consistent staff count throughout the day.

For ordering ice cream, we need to consider additional challenges. In this case, we're reliant on each store's storage capacity and the product's shelf life. Toppings and ice cream cones may spoil after a few weeks, necessitating more accurate forecasting than the ice cream itself.

Predicting specific ice cream flavour sales might be required, as demand varies based on the customer segment. For example, older customers may prefer coffee and bitter flavours, while children might favour strawberry and vanilla. To address this, we need data on customer demographics.

Determining the desired outcome of the forecasting solution is vital as it significantly impacts the requirements and costs. That's why you need to determine a single outcome. If you're tasked to develop "a forecasting solution," your primary responsibility is to request or identify a *specific* outcome. There's a systematic way to understand if you're solving the right problem.

CONNECTING WITH STRATEGY

An outcome needs to be clearly connected to the company's strategy. Many AI projects are funded as opportunistic endeavours for the technology and lack a clear purpose. When delving into the problem, part of the process is discovering the connection with the overall strategy. If no link can be found, the project might not be as viable as initially believed.

The discussion around outcome and strategy can't be initiated with the question, "Does this outcome and solution align with your overall strategy?" It isn't adequate to test for a connection. You could argue that almost any given outcome aligns with your strategy. Instead, asking, "How does this align with my overall strategy?" is a better way to investigate the valid strategic link.

No connection, no deal

In Paperflow, we initially tried to sell the idea of reading invoices to banks. Automating the book-keeping process, would also involve online banking services. We realised that many small businesses had to input invoice data into their online bank when paying bills and again into their accounting software for tax purposes.

Imagine if a bill could be paid by uploading the invoice to your bank. That would simplify the process, and for small businesses, the data could be available for export into the accounting software after payment. This could eliminate much of the manual work.

Small business owners typically pay bills weekly, while book-keeping is only necessary when taxes are due. As small business owners ourselves, we understood the problem. For us, the book-keeping process and bill payment operated reversely, as it was designed with the book-keeper's daily tasks in mind. First, the invoice is sent to the book-keeper, who enters it into the accounting software. Then, perhaps every other week, unpaid invoices are retrieved from the accounting software, uploaded to an online banking solution, and paid.

The problem is that bill payment has a time lag and requires manual intervention from the book-keeper. Reversing this process allows bills to be ready for payment at any time in the online bank, without needing manual entry. We finally had a no-brainer business outcome for our solution.

And it gets better.

One of Scandinavia's most prominent banks held an innovation competition with teams and employees from the bank only. We were involved because the winning team needed our service to build their solution. One team chose to build a prototype of this payment solution based on Paperflow and it won. We were thrilled as this could be a massive customer for Paperflow.

Sadly, we never made a deal with the bank. Although we discussed it with them, they declined. Improving the banking experience for their SMB clients wasn't a priority. They said there wasn't a "good business case in a better customer experience." It took years before banks started adopting the idea.

We wasted our time because of a lack of connection with a business outcome on the bank's side. The outcome of the solution was time saved for the bank's small business customers. The bank could have achieved higher customer satisfaction in this segment. But let's face it, the customer satisfaction of small business clients isn't a priority for large banks. Adding a solution like ours would require maintenance, getting clients support on board and risks. Banks aren't looking for more of that. Not for a low-priority business outcome like customer satisfaction.

That's why the idea never progressed. That is why many AI projects get stuck in beta. They are just not connected to a priority business outcome.

Smaller banks that prioritised customer satisfaction later adopted the solution.

UNDERSTAND THE PROBLEM DOMAIN

Having chosen an outcome, you must now dive deeply into the problem domain. To do this, you must first break down the problem domain into components that can be addressed systematically. Next, you must investigate how others have tackled similar issues, and finally, you must ensure that there's consensus on what the problem truly entails.

PROBLEM COMPONENTS

Understanding a problem in AI comes from investigating three main components:

Data

Data contains information on observed and recorded history. To understand a problem, you need to examine the available data so you can begin to form a hypothesis. Start by making sure you know the most fundamental premises. Revisit those you're confident you already know.

For the SundAI case, questions could look like these:

- How often is the given task solved today? This could refer to the number of invoices in Paperflow or forecasting frequency in SundAI.

- How many ice creams are sold, and what's the distribution between flavours?
- Do ice cream sales vary between stores based on flavours, time, or average sale size?
- What's the average price per sale?

Afterwards, you can work your way up the complexity scale. An example of a more complex question is: "What customer segment buys more ice cream per sale?" or, "What specific segment buys at a specific time of month".

The problem is that many people go straight to the complicated (often more interesting) questions as they want to crack the complex problems.

It's best to start with simple questions as they often provide the showstopper answers. For example, if the number of invoices is unknown, that's a problem, and more complex questions won't matter until it's answered. If the domain expert's answer conflicts with the data, there's either a fundamental data issue or a fundamental perception issue. That needs to be understood before you can move on to more complicated questions.

You might be surprised by some findings and will need to discuss them with domain experts for clarification. You need to investigate if there's a significant discrepancy between their responses and the data. Perhaps the experts are biased, or the data quality is low.

Domain experts

At Paperflow, we had a sign on the door to the developer's room. It said: "In God we trust – all others must bring data." It made sense for a data-driven company like ours and underlined that we didn't make decisions without looking at the data first. Today, I'd prefer a sign saying: "In God we trust – all others must bring users."

Data is evidence, but the eyewitness accounts from users and experts allow us to connect the dots. Therefore, we must interview and observe domain experts and users in their work to understand the problem being addressed.

Self-explorations and testing

A straightforward approach to grasping a problem is to perform the task manually. This will reveal to you many unusual situations and subproblems that require attention.

UNDERSTANDING THE PAPERFLOW PROBLEM

When working with the book-keepers, we should have examined the broader context of the users work and considered how they would use the AI's results. It would have been beneficial to deeply investigate the book-keeping process, related systems like enterprise resource planning, and task differences among book-keepers. In hindsight, we could have accomplished this by asking about the following:

Identify variations in user requirements

- Do accounting software applications always require the same data?

Accounting programs aren't uniform and may use different names or definitions for comparable data. A "reference number" in one application might be divided into two data points in another, and some may have open data entries for bookkeepers to use as they wish.

Most systems are designed for human input. Humans can easily adapt to varying requirements or definitions, but this can often be challenging for AI solutions.

How predictions will be used

- What additional processes will users undertake after reviewing the invoice data provided by the AI?

Paperflow users had diverse procedures. Some needed to match vendors to a list, while others wanted to split lines on invoices to different accounts. Approvals from colleagues were necessary in some cases, and the payment status of invoices varied. This meant that accounting couldn't be automated solely by reading invoices, as the data needed differed from one case to another.

Consider potential obstacles to automation

- Do the users require a manual review of AI results, and why?

Some users wanted to examine the invoice data even after our team had verified it. This apparently allowed them to understand better the business they were book-keeping for, which was essential for other purposes. As a result, no full automation was possible as the users insisted on a manual process.

Examine accuracy requirements

- What level of accuracy is acceptable for the AI, and how precise are book-keepers in their work?

We didn't grasp the requirements early on because we didn't investigate them thoroughly, so we lacked a specific accuracy target.

Explore the necessity and reasons for demanded predictions

- Which data fields (amounts, dates, etc.) from the invoices did customers require, and why?

Data needs varied considerably among Paperflow users, depending on their preferences, the ERP system, and company guidelines. Since we didn't understand the rationale behind the requirements, we couldn't differentiate between nice-to-haves and need-to-haves. As with any product development, being unaware of the fundamental reasons for product features can make you a victim of user requests. While user requests may seem crucial in their own minds, probing into and understanding their necessity often reveals that a significant portion is of little value. By recognising this, you can conserve effort while still delivering an excellent solution.

In the case of Paperflow, we discovered the answers to these questions only after building the solution. A more in-depth investigation of the problem before AI development would have saved us considerable time.

USE WELL-KNOWN FRAMEWORKS

When investigating your problem, it's worth using established tools and frameworks. Since AI might be a novel concept for many project participants, employing familiar frameworks can make the new aspects more manageable. I often use frameworks like SWOT, brainstorming, Graphic Gameplan, and popular tools like Miro. However, introducing too many new elements with AI may risk overwhelming stakeholders rather than providing them with guidance. The best approach is to use familiar frameworks and tools as far as possible.

HAS THE PROBLEM BEEN SOLVED BEFORE?

During the discovery phase, we may come across a problem that's already been solved – not only on a project level but also at the sub-problem level. For example, SundAI could rely on existing sources for local event data rather than gathering it themselves.

Even when you can't directly use other solutions, you may still draw inspiration from them. Research articles often detail data collection methods, the amount of data used, and the performance of their models. This can help you to set realistic expectations for your own project. You can also find case studies from other companies with similar challenges online and reach out to them for further insights.

I recently listened to a podcast featuring a guest from a large Danish company discussing their AI implementation. Surprisingly, the guest revealed they were building a solution for scanning invoices to automate accounting – basically, replicating Paperflow. The team consisted of five people, and the company had a yearly volume of 600,000 invoices that could be processed through this solution.

This approach is unreasonable.

DO YOU AGREE ON THE PROBLEM?

A common issue in AI projects is the assumption that all participants are on the same page regarding the problem being addressed. In reality, they seldom are. Misalignment occurs in many AI projects, resulting in a solution satisfying only some stakeholders. You need to step back and ensure everyone is aligned on the problem and has investigated it enough to understand it fully.

Imagine a scenario in which stakeholders from the SundAI project convene to discuss a solution for their forecasting problem. Participants include the store, finance, and purchasing department managers. They meet to discuss a solution for their forecasting problem. Unbeknown to them, they each have different solutions in mind, which aren't addressed during the meeting because everyone assumes a forecasting solution can only be one thing. This situation is particularly common in AI projects.

Desired state exercise

The following exercise will help you synchronise stakeholders and involves three to six project participants, representing technology, customers or users, management, and domain expertise, describing their ideal resolution for the problem.

Instruct participants to write fifteen to twenty lines independently (without discussion). Allow participants twenty minutes to do this and emphasise the importance of prose over bullet points. (Bullet points tend to create a list of features rather than a cohesive statement.) The text should describe how they envision experiencing the solution six or twelve months from now, depending on the project's timeline.

A possible variation involves asking participants to adopt the end user's point of view.

Once they've finished, have each participant read their text aloud. It's likely they won't agree on the vision, as each participant writes from their unique standpoint. Technicians may emphasise technology, while domain experts focus on subject matter specifics. This remains the case even when writing from a user's perspective.

After this, the participants can discuss and agree on a common vision, that they document to avoid any potential misunderstandings later. If they can't agree, they can't build the solution.

USE A WORKSHOP TOOL

This step involves having the solution owner (possibly yourself) synthesise the texts into a single vision. Afterwards, discuss the shared vision to ensure everyone agrees. This vision should be read aloud, shared, and frequently referenced throughout the project, serving as the guiding principle.

You could use a tool for group interviews or workshops, such as the Miro online whiteboard. Tools like Miro offer two significant benefits. First, they provide an excellent digital platform for storing workshop information, user feedback, and more. In AI projects, it's common to receive abundant feedback and information from stakeholders and users. I used to rely on Post-it notes, but organising and maintaining their readability for months proved to be a nightmare. With everything stored in Miro, you can quickly revisit previous workshops and feed-back sessions while designing a solution.

The second advantage is that such tools facilitate input from domain experts during workshops. Group dynamics often include a mix of introverts and extroverts. Using a tool like Miro, you can engage every participant equally, not just those most outspoken.

ACQUIRING DOMAIN KNOWLEDGE THROUGH SUBJECT MATTER EXPERTS

Domain knowledge refers to the first-hand insights possessed by individuals experienced in the processes we aim to address.

In the case of SundAI, the ice cream buyer, store manager, cashiers, and accountants are domain experts. Even the customers are domain experts, whether or not they realise it. They may reveal what motivates them to buy ice cream. In Paperflow, domain expertise comes from accountants, business owners, book-keepers, and ERP-system vendors.

In the AI industry, domain knowledge is a vital component, and, "remember to consult domain experts," is a standard piece of advice. For generative AI this is even more crucial. So, how do we obtain the most valuable information from these experts effectively? Simply talking to domain experts doesn't guarantee they will provide complete, unbiassed, information. Without a systematic approach, you risk missing critical data or encountering misinformation.

Consider the various interests at play when interacting with domain experts. They may be your current or potential clients, which can motivate them to push you in a specific direction. Even more powerful forces can impact the information they provide, such as their egos creating bias, their current situations influencing their focus, and their innate desire to please others. This makes obtaining accurate domain knowledge difficult. Acquiring domain knowledge is as demanding as any technical skill and needs to be approached with the same level of diligence.

DATA IS ONLY HALF THE STORY

Some individuals working in AI will argue that domain knowledge isn't crucial when data is available. They believe that simply analysing the data will yield the necessary insights, while involving people can be messy and create noise. Creating AI solutions without allowing for this mess will be the foundation of a problematic launch instead of the first steps to success.

Data often tells only half the story. Gaining a thorough understanding of the data, its origins, and the reasons behind it is as essential as obtaining the data itself. For example, SundAI's data may show actual ice cream sales numbers but not potential sales or reasons for deviations.

Domain experts also play a critical role in identifying relevant data sources. They may be aware of data sources, such as a local event calendar, that would have never occurred to you. Additionally, data is often collected with varying degrees of diligence. One ice cream store manager might meticulously record shift changes, while another might only remember occasional adjustments made on the fly. Relying on data without the input of domain experts can lead to a lack of insight, which may not become apparent until AI solutions are tested with users.

DOMAIN EXPERT INTERVIEWS

Interviewing experts plays a significant role in acquiring domain knowledge. The objective is to gain both tacit and implicit knowledge. Tacit knowledge refers to what "we know what we know," and can articulate, such as the number of daily customers at SundAI or who purchases the most expensive ice creams. We can't readily explain implicit knowledge, like riding a bicycle. Many decisions are based on implicit knowledge, like a store manager who may be unable to justify why they need additional staff. Developing or applying AI solutions requires facilitating the acquisition of both knowledge types, which is done through meticulously designed interviews. Failure to do so can result in wasted time for you and the domain experts.

EXPLORING FEATURE ENGINEERING

A crucial purpose of interviewing domain experts is identifying the essential data features for your models. For example, if you're attempting to predict housing prices, consult a domain expert, such as a real estate agent, to pinpoint features that can help make accurate predictions. These features could include square footage, the number of rooms, and property locations, which are typically accessible through public databases of housing sales. However, some data may be more expensive or more complicated to obtain, such as previous owners' salaries or the quality of the floor plan. In this situation, there are two options: acquire the data regardless of the cost or rely on the domain experts to guide your selection of features. While the latter approach may be technically challenging, it can be less expensive.

IMPLICIT KNOWLEDGE

The challenge of interviewing domain experts to identify features lies in their abundance of implicit knowledge. Real estate agents, for example, may unconsciously pick up on signals while touring a house.

Nobel Prize winner and author of *Thinking, Fast and Slow* Daniel Kahneman refers to this as System 1 and System 2 thinking.[1] System 1 is fast and based on autopilot, while System 2 is deliberate and conscious thinking. Although it may seem counterintuitive, most of what experts do relies on System 1. Explaining System 1 thinking can be complicated, as it's simply just something they do.

Additionally, it's beneficial to interview both junior and senior domain experts. Juniors often rely less on autopilot and engage more frequently in System 2 thinking. When building AI, stakeholders often introduce you to the most senior domain experts to ensure you receive the best and most comprehensive knowledge. However, it's crucial to also meet with junior experts who are still questioning everything they do.

Text and images increase implicit knowledge

When building image or text models, feature engineering can be more elusive. For visual models, the features can be subtle. As humans, we can discern minute details from one another without consciously thinking about them. Consider describing the visual differences between a wolf and a dog; these distinctions can be so nuanced that they may be difficult to articulate.

Context plays a more significant role when interviewing domain experts for image models. For example, when predicting housing prices from images, a car parked in front of the house could influence a domain expert's property value assessment. Similarly, doctors evaluating MR scans for cancer may be swayed by external factors like the patient's age and habits. During the interviewing process, it's advisable to minimise these factors and provide as little background information as possible.

For text models, the challenge is even more significant. Texts, like images, can have hard-to-define features. Similarly, language also contains a wealth of interpretations, subtexts, and background knowledge, making it difficult to determine why one customer's email should be prioritised over another's. Background knowledge can vary significantly, so it's not uncommon for two close colleagues to have differing opinions about the precise meanings of words and phrases.

BEWARE OF BIAS

The bias of domain experts also adds complexity when conducting interviews. For example, a real estate agent might overemphasise the importance of a house's location due to a narrative perpetuated by the media or industry insiders. As a result, domain experts might provide inaccurate information without knowing or intending to.

In any field, commonly accepted beliefs may or may not be accurate. For example, at SundAI, it could be assumed that customers take more time choosing flavours at weekends than on weekdays. Similarly, the real estate industry might believe that a two-car garage significantly affects a house's price.

While these beliefs could be true, they might also be baseless folklore or outdated information resulting from past consumer behaviour. Often, these so-called truths relate to market trends and customer preferences, leading to statements like, "our customers prefer X" or, "the market will never accept Y." People often believe they know their customers better than the customers themselves.

Treat such statements as assumptions that require further validation through data analysis or user testing. Don't hesitate to document hundreds of such assumptions. Otherwise, relying on them could lead to building models or collecting data based on false premises.

INTERVIEW MORE EXPERTS

Always interview multiple domain experts to identify areas of disagreement and gain a more comprehensive understanding. Relying on the input of one expert may give a misleading perspective.

When discrepancies arise among domain experts, seize the opportunity to delve deeper. Encourage them to discuss their differing viewpoints, as this can reveal valuable insights into the intricacies of the domain.

Additionally, be aware that these varying perceptions among domain experts can serve as a warning of potential challenges during the implementation phase with users. Use these instances of disagreement to inform and develop training and communication strategies for users or customers of the solution.

EXPERTISE-INDUCED BLINDNESS

Expertise-induced blindness arises when experts who are aware of limitations in their field apply the same limitations to other areas, leading to false conclusions. For example, in the early 1940s the CEO of IBM is believed to have said, "I think there is a world market for about five computers." How could he have possibly overlook the opportunities and solutions that later materialised? He soon realised his prediction was wrong, making his company the leading computer manufacturer.

However, admitting your mistakes is not always easy for top executives, which is why entrepreneurs with little to no experience in a field can sometimes outperform established companies.

Always question whether limitations asserted by domain experts are valid. For example, during my time at Paperflow, experts believed that book-keeping could never be automated. However, many processes are automated today, and some companies even have no-touch accounting where certain invoices never require human intervention.

At SundAI, a store manager might insist that it's impossible to predict the number of daily customers, claiming that even two seemingly identical sunny Saturdays in mid-summer can yield vastly different results. They might say, "There's no way of knowing."

The principle to remember is: If an expert believes something is possible, it likely is. If they think it's not, it may still be possible—it's just a matter of how.

Therefore, record their perceived limitations as assumptions to be tested or researched later on.

INTERVIEW GUIDE

During the discovery phase of interviewing domain experts, focus on the business outcome and problem rather than the solution. Conducting useful interviews with domain experts requires planning and skilful techniques. To assist you, here's a list of helpful questions:

Question: Tell me about the last time you did X (e.g. forecast sales or planned shifts at SundAI).

This question is more effective than, "How do you forecast at SundAI?" The latter may elicit a polished, best-case scenario response that reflects how things are supposed to be done. People naturally want to present the best version of themselves and may hesitate to admit cutting corners or using workarounds in their busy work lives. However, real-life scenarios are mostly messy.

Teresa Torres provides an excellent example in her book *Continuous Discovery Habits*: When you ask how people buy jeans, they might say they prioritise brand and quality.[2] But when you ask about their most recent jeans purchase, they may reveal that they chose a pair because of a discount.

When applying AI solutions, you must identify these messy situations and procedural shortcuts, as they can present challenges. Addressing these issues with AI means you can deliver significant value.

Question: How do you plan to use the information provided by the AI solution (for example, data on daily ice cream sales)?

This question emphasises the business need and outcome rather than simply focusing on the desired information or technical solution. The actual value of any AI lies in the actions taken based on the information it provides. By exploring the intended actions, you can uncover the solution's potential value and gain insight into the rationale (or lack thereof) behind the need.

Question: How would the solution help a new colleague?

Experienced employees may struggle to see the potential benefits of assistance (from AI or otherwise), as they can often find solutions to challenges independently. However, when considering inexperienced colleagues, they may more readily recognise the value and explain how the solution could help.

Question: Why is AI the preferred solution to this problem, rather than other methods?

This question often leads the subject to explain how they think AI will address the problem, revealing potential misconceptions about capabilities and limitations. It also exposes the depth of thought put into the idea — is AI being chosen due to hype, or have alternative approaches been seriously considered? Don't hesitate to challenge the use of AI. By doing so, you can ensure stakeholders are confident in its application.

Question: Why might this solution fail?

You may have encountered situations where people claim, "I knew that would fail." If this sentiment holds, asking this question can help avoid potential issues. Additionally, you should acknowledge any feelings of overlooking challenges due to excitement about a solution—a feeling many may be familiar with.

Question: Can you demonstrate how you perform your task?

Ask the person to show you how they carry out their work. Observing their actions can reveal implicit knowledge that might not be evident from their verbal explanations. Aspects of their tasks that have become routine or automatic may be unclear to an outsider.

Question: What challenges do you foresee with (X, Y, and Z)?

Inquire about potential difficulties, such as, "What challenges might arise in achieving high accuracy?" or, "What obstacles could emerge while getting users on board with the solution?" Questions like these can uncover data features that may be less reliable than initially assumed. Responses such as, "We recently changed how we log data for X," are common in these situations.

Task: Define and document the adjectives

Encourage domain experts to provide explanations for the adjectives they employ. If a SundAI employee uses adjectives like "good" customer or "stressful" day, ask them to clarify their meaning. We often assume that the meaning of these words is universally understood, but is it?

For instance, does "good customer" refer to someone who orders expensive ice cream? A regular patron who consistently orders the same flavour? Or maybe someone who never complains?

Similarly, what constitutes a "stressful day"? A high volume of customers? Or perhaps the shop running out of strawberry flavour, leading to complaints?

Domain experts and project stakeholders frequently use terms like "important" in contexts such as, "The solution must identify important parts of the text." In cases like these, insist on obtaining a clear definition of what "important" means. The term must be connected to an action, as nothing is inherently important.

By examining these loaded expressions more closely, you can better understand the problem and develop an effective solution.

TESTING BEFORE BUILDING

The objective of the discovery phase is to ensure a thorough under-standing of the problem and to confirm the correct issue is being addressed. This can be challenging, as determining the efficacy of potential solutions can be difficult. We can't be sure of a solution's impact as there are too many moving parts. As AI – especially genera-tive AI – can have a vast outcome space, and we don't know how users will react to results, we can't determine its efficacy. One approach involves testing the solution before it's fully developed. Presenting mock AI predictions to potential users or domain experts can gather valuable feedback that would otherwise only be available after substantial development.

Fake AI predictions can be generated at various stages of a project. The most cost-effective method involves creating simulated results before any data or modelling work. These predictions can be generated randomly or created by a domain expert. For example, if attempting to predict water pipe leakage, you could first have an expert analyse water pressure data and provide their prediction. This prediction and any associated "certainties" can then be shown to your test subjects.

Alternatively, you can use the earliest possible prototype of a model. With AutoAI solutions, creating a model within hours is often possible. At this stage, accuracy isn't the primary concern. The aim is to explore how users will interact with the AI-generated information and address any questions or concerns.

SUMMARY

You're more likely to succeed in tackling the problem if you begin by questioning its scope and your understanding of it. After carefully investigating the domain and gathering relevant knowledge, you'll have enough information to shift your focus towards devising a solu-tion. You'll then be able to align stakeholders with the issue being addressed.

CHAPTER 8
DISCOVERY – DECISION MAKING AND ACCURACY

Let's repeat: AI produces predictions – information that (in a business context) generates no value in itself. The value comes from using the predictions to decide how to act.

For the next part of the discovery phase, the activities are:

- make a decision model
- set goals for accuracy
- draw up a solution design

THE EFFORT IN AI IS SKEWED

Often, a substantial amount of work goes into understanding the problem, collecting data, using training models and deploying them to provide a prediction. Big Tech spends more than $30 billion annually researching this technology alone. With so much effort going into generating potential value worldwide, no wonder we want to realise as much of that value as possible.

The value generated from AI models is affected by two main parameters:

- The accuracy of the prediction
- How well we use the prediction in decision-making

AI models generate predictions such as: *there's an 80% risk that a SundAI store will run out of vanilla ice cream tomorrow.* There's no business value in making that prediction without a decision to act (or not act). In my experience, most AI projects pay more attention to generating accurate predictions rather than using the output for sound decision-making.

Decision-making is the solution side of the discovery phase. By deciding how to use predictions, you can design business processes around the AI solution and the connections to other IT systems. In other words, you map out the *solution design*. You identify the exact information you need when you design the *decision model*. This might sound counter-intuitive, as many AI solutions are made by first making a prediction solution and then trying to add a decision layer. Designing predictions before decisions takes you down the road to disaster.

Decision-making is a distinct scientific field. (Google has a Chief Decision Scientist, showing how important it is.) Decision-making is half the equation in generating value with AI (the other half is machine learning). There's room for improvement. This is where you can make or break a business case. An AI model that produces accurate information is worthless without a thorough decision-making process. If any value is achieved, it's down to luck rather than skill.

Decisions make processes and solutions. You might even call a process a *nexus of decisions*. As a result, decision-making is how you design AI solutions. That is why decision-making is the other half of the discovery phase in this method.

DECISION MODEL

A way to make better decisions is to make a *decision model*. Here we're looking at predictive AI – we'll discuss decision modelling for generative AI below.

Your decision model links the AI predictions with the actions people should take. It's a framework that helps you to map out your decision options. It also works as a communication tool. Mapping out decisions in the discovery phase means you can determine what information (predictions) you need to make those decisions. For example, if SundAI wants to map out decisions on how many staff are needed on a given day, using information about the average amount of ice cream sold during a day is insufficient. They'll need predictions hourly to ensure enough staff for the day's peaks. The decision model makes it easier to work out the practical value of the predictions produced by the AI solution.

A decision model is a table of actions based on the AI model's predictions and *confidence* – the model's perception of how likely a prediction is to be true.

A decision model to predict whether a customer will accept a proposal could look like the following:

Prediction	Confidence	Action
Accept	above 80% and below 95%	send offer
Accept	above 95%	increase price by 10%
Decline	above 90%	stop spending time on offer
Decline	above 50% and below 90%	call client for more information

Table 11: Prediction

I've picked four action examples – we could add an endless number. Sometimes, actions are easy to agree on in a project group. At other times, it's a challenging and lengthy process that involves several stakeholders. Deciding on actions can be challenging when they affect many areas of the company. When SundAI plans shifts, the local manager might need to involve Human Resources and Finance. This can initiate extended discussions, and domain experts might disagree on the best actions given the predictions and their corresponding confidence.

GENERATIVE MODELS AND DECISION MODELS

Generative AI needs different decision models to predictive AI. The output of generative AI (often a text or image) doesn't come with a confidence score you can use for thresholding actions. The output can be anything. This means you can only build a decision model with one output and one action.

Generation	Confidence	Action
Support email answer (text)	-	A human reviews and sends

Table 12: Decision model

On the plus side, the decision model or process flow will get more straightforward, although there are challenges. Not knowing the quality of the output makes it challenging to create fully automated systems. As a result, the action is almost always a human review.

A confidence threshold is often set for predictive AI, and anything above that threshold triggers an automated action. For example, the above-mentioned accounting model could automatically act as a book-keeper if confidence was above 98%.

AI Agents making autonomous decisions

At the time of writing, the newest development in generative AI is agents that can act autonomously, including making decisions. For example, the open-source project Auto-GPT is based on models from OpenAI; ChatGPT and GPT-4. It can also use tools like accessing documents, the internet, and other external plugins. That enables AI-based agents to make decisions autonomously, leaving the otherwise easy-to-map decision model out of this solution.

AI agents have three primary components: the brain, the body, and the tools.

For example, let's consider the creation of an AI agent that functions as a salesperson. Imagine your business involves selling office supplies. You could design an AI agent capable of accepting customer orders, verifying product availability from a stock database, and responding to the customer with a quote. This agent would also have the capacity to identify any special contracts in place with the client and could peruse previous correspondence.

The brain: The brain is the LLM that does the reasoning. It takes the user's input, in this case an email from the client, identifies the products and looks up their prices and availability in the database. The brain is also able to look through previous correspondence if necessary. Should the agent do that? If the email includes a message such as, "I'd like to order the same products as last time," the agent should use that option. The brain does that reasoning and makes a decision.

The body: This code integrates the tools with the brain. The body can also connect to a memory so the LLM can remember more of the dialogue.

The tools: These are the solutions that the agent has access to. They could be a search engine, a database, an email client, or a document archive.

Decisions with AI agents

In the above example, the agent could use a tool (access to previous correspondence) or not use it. When a user prompts an agent for information, the decision would be to use its existing information to provide an answer or use a search engine or knowledge database to find the optimal response. These are all decisions that must be handled.

Even when an agent makes the decision autonomously, you still need to decide what action should be taken based on the output. For now, there's no way of knowing if the text contains something you'd deem unacceptable. There's always a slight chance that the quote sent to the customer is wrong or the text is discriminatory. For example, a language model could assume that a man is the decision-maker when both men and women are mentioned in a text.

That means that most companies need humans to review all output before use. Our fully automated office supply sales rep is still only a good idea.

Productively applying predictive AI involves making a decision model for mapping output, confidence, and actions. For example, you could take a classic churn model that predicts how likely a customer is to cancel their agreement (churn) with a company. Mapping out the actions to take given a prediction (churn or not churn) is the first step in building the solution.

No code or data acquisition should be undertaken if the decision model can't be made. The most common cause of AI solutions not going into production is that the business can't agree on the actions to take, given a prediction and an output.

Suppose the churn model predicts a customer has a 60% likelihood of churning in the next three months. How do you handle that? Do you provide a discount? Call the client? Simply accept it and use it as a forecast? As most businesses get stuck in strategic, legal, or other discussions, AI solutions never surpass a prototype. Too bad if you invest a lot of time and money in development and then disagree on how to use it.

But it's not easy to make a decision model for a solution based on generative AI. The model output isn't simple labels, such as churn or no churn. Instead, it's a piece of text or an image. At the same time, there's no confidence score. In this case, you can only build a decision model with one output and one action.

On the bright side, the decision model or process flow will get more straightforward, although it also creates challenges. As you don't know the quality of the output, and the output can be anything, it's tough to create fully automated systems. A confidence threshold is often set for predictive AI, and anything above triggers an automated action. For example, the above-mentioned accounting model could provide automatic book-keeping if confidence was above 98%.

One way to achieve something similar to a confidence score in generative AI is to use the models confined in the source material. Suppose you have an agent using a database of contract templates or support articles. Then you can get a confidence score on the model's certainty indicating that the source material was a good match or not, for the prompted request.

CONFIDENCE THRESHOLDS

Suppose an AI model predicts a customer will accept an offer with 80% confidence. Is that enough to send an offer with no further action? Why not 90% or 50%? Sometimes, there's no easy way to set the correct confidence level. You must select one and adjust it as you become experienced with the consequences.

At other times, confidence levels can be chosen based on a benchmark. In Paperflow, many clients automated the invoice process with 98.5% confidence in the data. It turned out that this level made users see the number of mistakes as negligible. That's in line with Google research showing people view speech-to-text as useless at 95% accuracy but useful at 98%. Seemingly small changes in accuracy can have remarkable consequences for user experience.

Benchmarks can also be based on human accuracy for a given task. Suppose you're building an email classifier and have measured that humans are 97% correct in classifying emails. A decision model could look like this:

Prediction	Confidence	Action
email class	above 97%	put email in class folder
all others	below 97%	leave for a human to classify

Table 13: Decision model

Beware, though. AI mistakes might differ from those made by humans, so accuracy is not always comparable. A human book-keeper might make a typing error when entering invoice data or misunderstand the invoice. These mistakes seem fair when other humans evaluate their work. When AI makes mistakes, it might seem like the AI is clueless. It's better to set the bar a little higher for AI when the benchmark is set for a human.

Finally, you need to consider the potential cost of a mistake. At SundAI, we should be able to calculate the cost of having too many or too few staff at the ice cream store. The cost of a book-keeping error might be harder to calculate.

Setting the confidence level is also a matter of the model action's impact. If the outcome of a wrong answer is a disaster, you might set very high confidence thresholds. Imagine a self-driving car that has an 80% threshold for the light to be green. It won't take many traffic lights before it crashes.

DECISION MODELS INCITE NEW MODELS

The sales-quote-predictor-AI has an "increase price by 10%" action in the decision model if the customer is more than 95% likely to accept the offer.

When designing decision models in AI, we sometimes discover the potential for additional models that could improve our solution or even be necessary for achieving our desired outcome.

Prediction	Confidence	Action
yes	above 95%	increase cost by 10%

Table 14: Desired outcome

Why add 10% to the price? Why not 20% or 5%? And why not train a model to predict the optimal price increase? The decision model clarifies your need to consider building a price optimisation model. But if you hadn't mapped out the decision model first, you might not have realised this until you were far into the project and had made your initial AI model.

YOU PROBABLY WANT MORE INFO

In general, mapping the decision model provides insights into the additional information you need to make rational decisions. SundAI needs to forecast how many customers they'll have so they stock enough ice cream. But as we map out this prediction with relevant actions in a decision model, it's clear that the number of customers isn't adequate information to make a decision. The local store manager might point out that children prefer vanilla and strawberry, and adults prefer more bitter flavours. To stock the correct ice cream flavours, we need to forecast the sales of each variant. That requires logging information on customer ages or collecting data about local events.

We need this information when we build a decision model, but if we first realise this *after* building the AI model, we're effectively back to the beginning.

OTHER TYPES OF MODELS

As described earlier, the sales order model is a tabular classification problem that uses building-block terminology. Regression and fore-casting models are different, as these outputs are a number and a deviation. That could be:

amount of ice cream sold on Friday: 145 (between 122 and 177 with 90% certainty).

The decision model is different but follows the same logic. It could look like this:

Prediction	Confidence	Action
150 ice creams or more	above 95% (with a range below +/- 20)	automatically call extra employee
149 ice creams or less	above 95% (with a range below +/- 20)	no action

Table 15: Decision model

DECISION LEVELS

When making a decision model, it's beneficial to discuss the *decision levels*, or in other words, the level of autonomy with which the model makes a decision. The higher the level, the more autonomous the decision-making.

You can make up and divide decision levels however you like. There's no specific standard. I often use the following:

LEVEL 1: WARN/INFORM

The least autonomous level is warnings or information. For example, when you're writing in Microsoft Word or Google Docs it warns you about possible errors by underlining what could be spelling mistakes. For SundAI, it could be an email with the expected amount of ice cream sales that day.

LEVEL 2: SUGGEST

For example, in Word, this could be the suggestion to correct a spelling mistake with the correct spelling shown. A suggesting decision level could also recommend a lower price if the AI model predicts a customer won't accept the proposal for purchase.

LEVEL 3: CONDITIONAL AUTOMATION

Conditional automation is a decision level that's implemented under certain conditions. These conditions could be certainty from the model, specific predictions, or external conditions.

For example, suppose a model predicts with 99% certainty that a word is spelt incorrectly. Given this condition, the word corrects automatically without user intervention. That's a certainty-based condition. A prediction-based condition is when the predicted label determines the action. Some words are commonly misspelt, and the decision model's creator might decide that the word *acheive* automatically becomes *achieve*. The condition here is that words with the predicted incorrect spelling are corrected without user intervention. Prediction-based conditions can also be a range, like automatically ordering additional ice cream if the prediction is sales of between 150 and 300 ice creams for a day.

External conditions might be the time of day. Suggestions might be provided to a manager during working hours, but they could be made automatically when no one is around to approve the decision.

These types of conditions can be combined.

LEVEL 4: AUTOMATIC

Automatic decisions are implemented without intervention, although humans can still stop, cancel, or change decisions if required.

For example, a self-driving car that tells you when to grab the wheel and steer manually uses an automatic decision-level system. You can let the car drive itself but still take over the wheel and override the decision-making.

SundAI could make the automated ordering of ice cream and call-in employees with the option of the manager later modifying decisions if things change or their experience tells them that a better decision can be made.

LEVEL 5: AUTONOMOUS

The highest decision level is autonomy. For example, with a self-driving car without a steering wheel, there's no option for a human user to intervene in the decision-making.

Entirely autonomous systems are rare, probably because they're risky to deploy. Most AI systems range from level 2 to 4 and provide plenty of value.

An example of an autonomous system with deadly outcomes was the Boeing 737 Max 8, which saw two crashes six months apart in October 2018 and March 2019. The crashes were due to a system that should correct the plane's pitch with no way for the pilots to intervene. In both cases, a sensor told the system the plane was ascending at too steep an angle while in fact, it was not. The autonomous system adjusted the tail elevators pressing down the nose to correct the assumed pitch, which otherwise could cause the plane to stall. Due to insufficient training, the pilots didn't know that a sensor failing could cause the correction and therefore tried to manually increase the pitch only to invoke another automatic adjustment which eventually made the plane dive and crash.

The discussions you have when going over decision levels with users and stakeholders are extremely valuable and shouldn't be omitted. Often, stakeholders have very different decision levels in mind without having a common language to discuss them. For example, SundAI's store managers could be cautious about automatically ordering ice cream based on predictions because they're responsible for potential consequences. At the same time, headquarters see a chance to increase revenue by having less lost business. Deciding on decision levels makes actions easier to agree on, as everyone understands the conse-quences.

CONFIDENCE AND ACCURACY

We make decisions based on information from AI's predictions. We evaluate the prediction on a conscious or unconscious level depending on how much we can trust it. In AI, that trust relies on a two-layered interpretation of prediction confidence.

First, how high is the prediction confidence? If the model is very confident, we can trust it more. What entails high confidence differs from case to case.

The second layer is how much we can trust the model's confidence score, based on its perception of how likely a prediction is to be correct. It can be very accurate or wildly inaccurate.

The accuracy of models and the confidence of predictions are strongly connected with decision-making. The challenging part is settling on what accuracy is sufficient for the solution to fulfil its purpose. After that, the discussion often turns to what confidence score we can use to make specific decisions and activate each decision level.

Perceptions of high accuracy or trustworthy confidence can be very individual. The finance manager at SundAI might be proud to be a precise worker, setting the bar high for accuracy and confidence. The store manager might be used to hectic work with mistakes happening constantly and have lower accuracy expectations. Agreeing on a decision model will be much more difficult if you don't identify these different perspectives.

ACCURACY AND CONFIDENCE ARE NOT THE SAME

There's a distinction between accuracy and confidence. *Accuracy* is the general average chance of the model making the correct prediction, while *confidence* is the model's perception of the chance a given prediction is correct.

A model might be 99% accurate on average but have 55% confidence on an individual prediction level. More accurate models usually provide more confident predictions, but you should be prepared to handle low-confidence predictions even with a very accurate model.

ACCURACY VALUE

In Paperflow, the accuracy of the AI was an important consideration for potential customers. The first question everyone asked was, "How accurate is the AI?" By that, people meant the accuracy of reading the invoices' data fields. After a while, we learned that accuracy didn't matter as much for the clients as we'd – and they had – thought.

Accuracy matters when it comes to business value. However, the difference between 90% and 95% correct results was less significant than expected, and user feedback was almost the same in both cases.

That became even clearer when we went head-to-head with competitors. Being five or even ten percentage points better than a competitor wasn't always enough to win a client. Many factors are more critical than accuracy, with ease of implementation and price at the top of the list. Paperflow needed to achieve high accuracy to realise it was less significant than we'd originally thought. Often, the model's accuracy isn't the strategic advantage you need to beat your AI competition or create optimal solutions.

AGREE ON HOW YOU MEASURE ACCURACY

Answering, "How accurate is the AI?" wasn't as straightforward in Paperflow as you might think, and that challenge isn't unique.

First, the clients had wildly different invoices regarding layout and readability, there was no "average" invoice. Small Danish companies, mostly buying from other small Danish companies, received invoices with a clean design from their modern accounting software, all delivered as PDFs. Transport and logistic companies (the worst in invoice readability) had invoices with much information specific to that sector, making them hard to read, even for humans. The invoices were often printed, stamped with handwritten notes added, and scanned before Paperflow received them for processing. Providing average accuracy numbers wasn't helpful to anyone.

At the same time, there were different ways of calculating the accuracy. We initially did so by counting the number of data fields (amounts, dates, etc.) correctly scanned on a set of invoices and dividing that number by the total amount of fields.

Say we had 100 invoices with five fields to read on each. That's 500 fields. With 450 of these correctly read by the AI, the accuracy would be $450/500*100 = 90\%$. Some customers agreed with that calculation, but others measured the accuracy by dividing the amount of entirely correctly read invoices by the total amount. A set of invoices showing 90% accuracy when calculating by field could easily be 50% accurate when calculating per invoice – especially if clients had 15 or even 20 fields per invoice. Having promised 90% accuracy to a customer who experiences 50% isn't beneficial to user satisfaction.

Agreeing on how to measure the accuracy of an AI solution is the first goal on your path to a helpful decision model. However, it might not be as simple as choosing between different ways of calculating accuracy as we did in Paperflow.

If you don't start by agreeing on what accuracy means, there's a risk of the entire solution not being a good fit for the users. This could mean having to go back and redesigning the solution, including models and training data.

NOT ALL INFORMATION IS EQUAL IN VALUE

Some predictions from a given model can be more valuable than others. For example, at SundAI, predicting the exact amount of ice cream sold can vary in value. It might not matter to be exceptionally accurate as long as the prediction of the number of customers is within a particular range. Suppose a single employee in the ice cream store can serve up to 20 customers per hour. In that case, predicting the number of customers from a model lower than 15 doesn't require high confidence. Whether there are 5 or 15 customers per hour will require the same number of employees. But as soon as the number is close to 20, the prediction is critical information that calls for extra staffing.

Now, the value increases, and prediction accuracy becomes more critical.

You can quickly end up with a model that accurately predicts the number of customers for most scenarios but doesn't identify valuable information. Most data we collect follows a bell curve. You've probably seen a curve representing the spread of IQ scores. Most people have an IQ close to 100, while both much higher and much lower IQs become increasingly rare. A lot of data for AI works like that. The number of customers per hour at SundAI might concentrate around 12, while less than two or more than 30 is extremely rare.

The value in the SundAI model is only realised when we can accurately predict more than 20 customers per hour, but that's a rare case. The model could be 98% accurate and never provide this valuable information. The AI discovery phase should identify what predictions are valuable. And when gathering training data and investing effort into making optimal decisions, the effort should focus on the most valuable portions of the prediction spectrum.

PERCEIVED ACCURACY

At Paperflow, we shifted to measuring perceived quality. The goal was no longer an exact percentage of accuracy. Instead, we relied on customer feedback to judge the quality. That might seem obvious in hindsight, but the initial user feedback was that accuracy was paramount. This is common for AI solutions.

We'd often deploy a new and better model that we knew through careful measurement provided more accurate predictions, and still receive negative feedback. Users asked, "What did you do? The accuracy is suddenly worse!" We carefully tested to make sure the accuracy was higher on the new deployment than the previous one, and it was. The accuracy was undeniably better.

After much dialogue with the users, we realised that when improving the model, some wrong predictions were repaired while new mistakes were added. On average, we made more fixes than mistakes, resulting in higher accuracy on paper. But that was different from what the users perceived. They no longer saw the existing fixed errors, while the new ones were very apparent. They made the accuracy seem lower.

As humans, we tend to accept known mistakes and grow comfortable with them. When they get fixed, we barely notice. But new mistakes stand out. Significant quality improvement was needed to outweigh the newly introduced errors. It also meant waiting for longer intervals before releasing new versions to users would provide higher perceived quality. Delaying updates was against our policy of deploying often, as we wanted to provide improved accuracy as soon as possible. Perceived quality made us change that habit.

Evaluating prediction quality doesn't have to be quantitative. It doesn't always reflect the accuracy seen from a user perspective. User experience always beats quantitative measurements. Even if model accuracy must be sacrificed, it's always the better option.

WHO ARE YOU TRYING TO BEAT?

There were once two men walking on a savannah in Africa. They met a sizeable hungry lion that had sneaked up on them. The two men had no chance of getting away. One of the men laced up his shoes. The other said, "You can't outrun the lion."

"I don't have to," answered the first. "I just have to outrun you."

That anecdote is a helpful guideline for how to look at accuracy in AI. When is the accuracy sufficient? If we step back and re-evaluate our actions with the decision model, might the acceptable accuracy change?

Agreeing on what accuracy is sufficient for solving a specific business problem is mostly a matter of perspective. You might find yourself being one of the two men on the savannah. This often happens when a group tries to set a goal for an AI solution's accuracy. Some turn to competing solutions whether they're comparable or not. Others compare it to the current situation, while a number compare it with an emotionally founded perception of the world. The latter is typical for domain experts and something I experienced in Paperflow. When asking book-keepers what accuracy would be sufficient, many instantly replied 100%, saying things like, "We don't make mistakes," or, "Our job is to do correct book-keeping that our clients can trust." When checking book-keeping transactions, we found plenty of errors. Still, book-keepers perceived their work as flawless.

Professionals misjudge their accuracy. They're like craftsmen. *Who did this terrible job?* is their first reflection when seeing something they didn't do. As a developer, I did that. I looked at the code and thought, *Who wrote this junk?* On checking, I often realised it was my code. I'm probably not the only developer who's had that experience. We tend to overestimate the quality of our work and underestimate that of others.

There will be many different experiences of the criterion for successful accuracy, so it's essential to get aligned.

First, we need to clarify the status quo. Get the project participants to agree on the current quality of human work. Never start the accuracy discussion by asking *what's sufficient accuracy.* Identify the status quo first.

We tend to set a *golden bar* for new technology. If the new AI solution can't solve all our problems, well, it just isn't good enough. To combat the golden bar problem, you can estimate the cost of accuracy compared with the benefit. A simple cost-benefit calculation, like the one shown below, will make that clear. The cost of accuracy is exponential. No AI can become 100% accurate, and the closer you want to get, the closer the price gets to infinity.

THE VALUE IS IN THE DECISION

The business case of any AI solution stands and falls with decision-making. Yet I often see minimal effort put into the decision-making framework compared to the effort into getting accurate predictions.

Information and predictions alone have no value in a business context. For example, the information that SundAI has a 90% chance of selling out of vanilla ice cream before closing on the following Monday has no value unless associated with an action. Nor does the information that a customer has a 75% risk of cancelling their membership on our platform within three months. Information is worthless unless it leads to action.

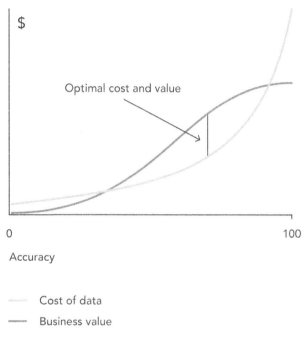

Figure 9: Optimal cost

DECISIONS FIRST – ALWAYS

Developing your decision model should come first. People working on an AI solution often make decisions about actions at a late stage, usually in the development phase or early in the implementation phase.

Those who haven't worked with AI before wonder if front-loading decision making is really necessary. They ask if they can wait until the models are built, and they can see the predictions. Once the predictions are visible and tangible it's easier to imagine them as the basis for specific actions.

However, you must firmly maintain the need for order prescribed here.

Creating your decision framework in the discovery phase may be costly in time and budget, but it is worth the effort. Postponing it means an incomplete discovery phase; the solution design must be significantly reworked. Building the decision framework late in the development phase will be expensive. You've already scoped the solution, interviewed domain experts, made a UX design, gathered data, labelled data, coded an end-to-end flow, and trained and evaluated the necessary AI models. If you then make your decision model, you might need different predictions to those you expected.

For example, SundAI could build an AI solution that predicts the number of customers for each store so they can stock up on ice cream. They get data from the point-of-sale terminals and the ERP system. Then they clean and prepare the data and develop their models. They show outstanding performance in their prediction accuracy.

But SundAI made the mistake of not building the decision model first. Ordering the correct amount of stock (action) based on the number of customers (prediction) is more complex than they expected. A local store manager is asked to make decisions.

"How much of each ice cream flavour, how many waffles, and how much topping do we need per customer?"

"That depends," says the manager. "Some days, we have children from local events coming by. They prefer flavours such as strawberry, and they prefer waffles. On other days, the customers are older and prefer other flavours served in a cup."

That new information shows we need to know the number and type of customer. That requires new models and new data. Neither the ERP nor point-of-sales will tell us who the customers are. SundAI now needs data on local events or maybe a model that predicts sales of each food item.

BUILD THE BUSINESS CASE ON DECISIONS

Since the value comes from decisions, the business case is based on these. Thus, you should use the decision model as the basis for your business case.

The decision model maps on the value side of the business case. You can use five variables for calculating the value of an AI solution:

1. model accuracy
2. action value
3. decision quality
4. volume
5. luck

For each action, the product of these variables constitutes the total value of one occurrence of an action.

Model accuracy: The more accurate the AI model is, the more you can tap the potential value. Suppose SundAI's model for forecasting ice cream sales is 90% correct while humans are 85% correct. In that case, the value should be found in the five added percentage points.

Action value: Each action has a value. If the salespeople who use the offer prediction model either save time on the sales process or make better decisions, there's value in that. The value of the action is often based on assumptions and is subject to debate, but that's no different to other business case processes. This parameter includes how well the solution is adopted by users, as discussed earlier.

Decision quality: This is defined by deciding on the optimal confidence threshold for the given action and how helpful it is towards the business outcome you're trying to achieve.

Volume: The number of times the AI is used also has a part in the equation. In Paperflow, the solution needed a certain volume of invoices to collectively achieve enough savings in time compared to entering the invoices by hand.

Luck: No matter what knowledge, experience, or effort went into making the decision, an element of luck will affect the value of your AI solution.

With these parameters, we can set the formula:

Model accuracy * Action value * Decision quality * Volume * Luck = AI value

The formula doesn't make a business case an exact science. But it does make it more tangible and should make you appreciate the AI business case's potential shortcomings.

Without a decision model, any project is a gamble.

The actions directly link the model and the desired business outcome. You can only know the value if you commit to specific actions. Even worse, deciding on actions after the development phase might mean you must rework data and modelling. That's why the ability to commit to a decision model is the best indicator to predict if an AI project will end in a successful solution.

I've sometimes declined to progress in an AI project, because the client wanted to skip mapping decisions before building models. For example, a client asked us to make an AI solution for internal use. The project participants were unwilling to work on a decision model before having built the model. Instead, they wanted to see the results before deciding how to use it. A call turned into a heated discussion, and the client decided to have another agency build the solution. A month later, I visited the client, and the leading role pulled me aside, telling me: "We built the solution, but we disagree if it works or not. Is that due to the lack of a decision model?"

It was.

The discovery phase activities are either something you do on purpose before building models or something you're forced to do after the fact. The latter results in delays, changes of scope or a project stalemate.

DECISION FLOWS

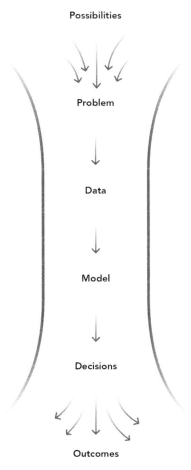

Figure 10: Decision flow

When you decide to build an AI solution, you do so from several opportunities. These opportunities can be issues to solve or potential for improving your business towards a given outcome. And from these opportunities, you select a problem to solve.

Once you've done that, you can start gathering data to train an AI model. If the data is good, you can make a model that provides accurate information. The information is now used for decisions that are either actions or inactions

143

These actions have business outcomes. Business outcomes can, for example, be money saved on avoiding having too many employees at work in the SundAI stores. Or it could be more sales as they didn't run out of ice cream. If the decision-making is high quality, you'll likely see better outcomes. But everything from selecting the best opportunity, defining the problem correctly, data collection, modelling and decision-making impacts the outcome. On top of this, an element of luck plays into the outcomes. Luck is a significantly underestimated part of successful outcomes.

The flow illustrates that you can't work on data and modelling alone, as is the typical approach. The flow is a chain that's no stronger than its weakest link. You have a weak or missing link if you put no effort into decision-making. One weak link, and you're likely to be disappointed with the outcome.

ELEMENT OF LUCK

Luck is especially present between the decision and outcomes. It always plays into the outcome, and you can't blame the outcome alone when retrospectively judging your decisions. You can experience very unfavourable outcomes with the right problem, data, modelling, and decision-making. And the opposite can happen. If you measure the outcomes alone, you might abandon or stay with a project for the wrong reasons.

Research shows that luck is a significantly underestimated part of success.[1] The media often interviews successful people on what made them so successful. The answers vary from hard work, strategic thinking or lessons learned early in life. The fact is that many other people did the hard work, thought strategically, and learned plenty along the way, but didn't come out on top. When researchers simulate the importance of luck and luck is given only 10% weight in the outcome role, it turns out that nine out of the top ten people with a great outcome were lucky.

The effect of luck matters in AI solutions as the value of implemented models is judged by their outcomes. The result is that AI solutions are either judged too positively or too negatively, as people vastly underestimate luck. The phenomenon is also known in psychology as *survivorship bias*. We retrospectively judge a solution based on the outcome, ignoring if the odds played in our favour or against us.

MAP THE FLOW

Mapping the decision flow will significantly help you and other project stakeholders to identify the shortcomings of or possible reasons for good and bad outcomes.

Figure 11: Mapping the decision flow

The primary function of mapping the flow is aligning with the objectives you aim to achieve. It also tells you which outcomes to measure.

DECISION-MAKING IS COMPLICATED

DECISIONS ARE FEELINGS

Neuroscientist Antonio Damasio has shown us that all decisions are based on emotions. He demonstrated this phenomenon through the story about Elliot.

After a brain tumour, Elliot completely lost the ability to make decisions. Initially, Damasio was perplexed. Elliot's IQ was normal, he could speak, reason, and make rational conclusions like any other mentally healthy person. Yet, he could not plan more than a few hours ahead, and simple decisions at his work, such as whether documents should be sorted by title or date, took several hours.

This is where Damasio had an epiphany. It's not the part of intelligence we know as the ability to reason, calculate, or discern patterns that govern decision-making. It is solely emotions. One might be tempted to think that a man without emotions would be extremely efficient and get things done quickly. But without any emotions to form preferences, goals, and motives, there are no decisions. No decision leads to chaos and apathy.

And here it becomes relevant for AI, because the technology does not have emotions or motives and is not going to get them. That's also why, as said earlier, AI is a poor name. Intelligence is much more than reasoning and rational conclusions.

It explains why decision-making is complex, especially in organisations driven by many people's feelings. When emotions are the basis for all decisions, it no longer makes sense to talk about objectively right and wrong decisions. Stakeholders have different ideas about the right decision based on the same information.

At SundAI, knowing that the optimal number of employees on Saturday is five might not result in a decision of five. It may feel like too few people to the store manager on a Tuesday. HR might think we've been asking for too much over time and running the risk of burnout. Finance might agree on five being correct, but as an unexpectedly large electricity bill just arrived, it feels better to cut costs and go with four.

Decision-making isn't a simple numbers game or an entirely rational exercise. It's also storytelling that must speak to both hearts and minds. You'll be disappointed if you go into a decision-making process with only numbers and rationales. Building the decision model for an AI solution happens in a nexus of emotions, which makes the process challenging.

KAHNEMAN HAS A POINT

The decision model should be built in the discovery phase with project stakeholders. A typical behaviour is that stakeholders try to avoid and postpone this discussion, even though I stress the importance of doing it early. The reason, I suspect, is to be found with Daniel Kahneman.

Kahneman's System 1 thinking works automatically with little or no effort. Driven by intuition and fast decision-making, we use it for 98% of our decision-making. System 2 comprises deliberate decision-making, where we take time to analyse the available information, consider alternative decision options and pick the one most likely to become successful. There's a time and place for both. System 1 makes us fast and efficient and uses little energy. After initial training, System 1 allows us to drive a car while relaxed. If we had to rely on System 2, we wouldn't get anywhere, and the activity would be exhausting.

When I ask project stakeholders to make a decision framework, they must use System 2 for something that may or may not happen sometime in the future. Most people prefer postponing such activities as they're already saving energy for the other System 2 decisions, they'll have to make that day.

The preference is often subconscious. People are unaware that they are cutting corners and acting on intuition. They'll try to avoid decision-making and, as a result, build a decision model. Don't let them. The decision-making must be done. By postponing it, the costs increase as decision-making might delay project completion.

DECISIONS ARE AFFECTED BY POLITICS, COMPLIANCE AND STRATEGY

Turning information (predictions in AI) into decisions is challenging because this is where we often meet politics, compliance, strategy, and as you now know - emotions. Management, the legal department and other parts of the organisation won't make much noise about the predictions (information) your AI has generated. But when you want to make decisions and take action, then everyone suddenly has an opinion.

Suppose you're heading the service and support department of a company building machines for other companies. With AI, you now want to predict the maintenance needs of the clients. Everyone will tell you "That's great" and move on. But once you start making decisions, you're in for another game.

Everyone else wants to get involved if you decide to pre-emptively contact clients. Marketing wants a say in how you communicate the activity. Legal wants to discuss how the warranty is affected when the company, not the client, initiates the issue. The sales department wants to discuss how this affects the strategy of replacing the older product line. Management will question the accuracy of the information. You'll be asked, "How certain are you that the machine will fail?", "What if you're wrong?", "What data are you using to train the AI?" and similar questions.

Suddenly, you're in for months of stakeholder management and possibilities for deadlocks. Management is the worst, saying things like, "We'll need to discuss this at the next leadership seminar in the fall." That's the death blow to any AI solution. Settling on a decision model in the discovery phase and not after building models will uncover potential issues and give you time to involve the right stakeholders in your initiative. You'll be prepared for these questions.

SUMMARY

The accuracy and quality of AI-solutions aren't always as simple as they might look. There's a big element of interpretation, feelings, and irrational human thinking in play. The most crucial aspect of working with quality and accuracy is to align with stakeholders and users. At the same time, the goal should never be to raise a number in accuracy. It should be to increase user satisfaction.

The information generated from AI has no independent value. The value is in the decisions and action that results in business outcomes. Putting effort into decision making will pay off.

All the hard decisions are made in the discovery phase. However, there are plenty of tools and methods to help you make those decisions and understand the problem. AI methods simply saying you need to "understand the problem" and leaving the way to do that up to the reader miss the point.

For many AI solutions, the time invested in the discovery phase can easily be 40% of the total project time. With generative AI that often has less data acquisition and less code than predictive AI, that number can be even higher.

CHAPTER 9
DATA HANDLING

When we founded Paperflow, I assumed data collection would be a matter of weeks or, at most, a few months of work for a few people. That turned out to be wrong. At one point, almost fifty people worked full-time to label the data we needed to train the models reading invoices.

Years and many optimisations later, Paperflow still has significant staffing to collect data. We ended up selling a premium product with manually validated data to generate revenue from the activity. Still, it was a significant and critical operation that I'd grossly underestimated.

Some AI solutions require an astonishing amount of data. At other times, you need little or no data. The goal in the data handling phase is to collect and use the correct data at a price that the business case can justify. But first and foremost, the fundamental principle in this phase is for the data to represent the real world and that should be considered before any activity and decision.

ACTIVITIES IN THE DATA HANDLING PHASE

The activities of the data handling phase are:

- collecting data
- labelling and cleaning data
- analysing and understanding data
- settling on data quality and amounts
- handling personal data issues

In this phase, you establish the data needs and routines to collect, label and analyse it. For many AI solutions, these activities continue throughout the solution's lifetime. That will turn the activities less exploratory and more production oriented.

GOAL OF THE DATA HANDLING PHASE

As stated, the goal in the data handling phase is to collect and use the correct data at a price that the business case can justify. If the data costs are too high, closing the project at this point is a viable option. Too many AI projects continue through data collection to model building, even though the cost of data is too high.

The business case of an AI solution can also change during this later production phase as the cost and needs for data change. The trend in AI is that we need less and less data, so for many solutions, the business case improves over time. That also counts for those you might have disregarded earlier.

For some solutions, the costs will go up as new data sources are necessary to keep the AI predictions at the accuracy found to be required in the discovery phase.

DATA TERMINOLOGY

We've already discussed data as a part of the building blocks. The data is in a spreadsheet format in *tabular data* building blocks, such as regression and forecasting. We have written text in *language* building blocks. In *vision,* we have images and videos. In *audio,* we have recorded sound files. But formats are just one side of AI data. Data comes in different distributions, combinations, and sizes, and to have a productive conversation on that, we need a common terminology.

Here are the most common terms in the vocabulary used in AI.

Dataset: A collection of data needed for training a model.

Data engineering: The task of making data available. That can be an immense task that can take months or years. Data engineering is often confused with data science. A data scientist's job is to understand, analyse and model data for business or research purposes. A data engineer's task is to build data pipelines and storage solutions to make data available cost-effectively. Both roles have some overlapping skills but usually not enough to substitute for each other.

Data cleaning: Data often comes from sources not created with AI in mind. The data comes in many formats. For example, *dates* can be written as free text, such as "October 18th, 2022" in some places and as "22-10-18" (YY-MM-DD) or "18-10-2022" (DD-MM-YYYY) in others. Before training AI models, we must harmonise (clean) the formats.

Transformations: When training tabular AI models, we often must provide the algorithm with a data type for each feature. That type is called transformation and can be *categorical, image, sound, numeric, timestamp* or *text.* The algorithm uses it to interpret the data when building the model.

Distribution: The amount of data points for each label in a dataset is rarely equal. You might only have ten images of poodles, but a thousand images of German Shepherds in a dog species dataset. The term "distribution" in AI is often used to explain these potential differences in amounts of data per label.

Data manipulation: The task of preparing data through modifications to make it ready for AI training. Perhaps we have a feature called *height* that could have the value "6'2" (meaning 6 feet, 2 inches).

Handling the data in separate feet and inches features or converted to centimetres is easier.

Noise: Noise is data points in a dataset that are random or meaningless. It can also be outliers (rare cases providing a wrong signal) or even false data due to either fraud or irrational behaviour.

Data operations: The activities associated with storing, maintaining, and making data available.

THE GOAL OF DATA IS TO REPRESENT THE WORLD IN WHICH THE AI SHOULD WORK

As stated in the opening of the chapter, representing the real world is a fundamental principle that needs to be considered before any activity and decision in the data handling phase. For SundAI, the data must reflect customer behaviour, preferences and the dynamics that drove sales for the ice cream stores.

But how do we achieve this goal?

PERFECTION IS IMPOSSIBLE

We perceive the world subjectively – that's what we call *bias*. We rarely agree on how to interpret it.

It doesn't even take two different human beings to get different world perceptions. In his book, *Predictable Irrational,* Dan Ariely illustrated how little stimulus humans need to change their views. In an experiment, Ariely divided the test subjects into two groups. One was asked to state two random numbers and the other the last two digits of their social security number. Then they were both were asked to name a fair price for performing a task. The latter group's prices were closer to their social security numbers than chance allowed.[1] This tiny anchor considerably altered the subject's understanding of a reasonable price, even though they were traders who were supposed to look rationally at numbers and prices for a living.

Another reason is that data is *recorded observations*. An event or measurement has taken place and been recorded in some way. Representing the world through recorded observations has two main challenges.

Firstly, we can't observe and collect all the relevant data. At least not at a practical price point. As an example, getting access to data about *all* SundAI's potential customers' current sentiments on ice cream and their whereabouts would increase the domain representation. However, that's just not possible.

Second, our observations are limited by how we make measurements. All measurements have some inaccuracy. For example, perfectly measuring the temperature of a glass of water is impossible as the temperature is affected by the thermometer. In the same way, customer satisfaction is affected when we ask them how satisfied they are with our products. It can be slightly increased as they see the inquiry as a positive effort.

HOW TO HANDLE IT

In AI, we can never know how far our data is from the perfect representation. We can't measure it because we don't know what perfect is. We can measure how well our models perform, but that's a part of the following phase of the method presented by this book. We can, however, deploy a range of initiatives and approaches to still make data useful.

Domain experts

Explain your insights and learnings from data to domain experts. If you were building the forecasting model for SundAI, you might learn that the average amount of ice creams per sale is 2.5. Or that the busiest day is Friday. A domain expert (a cashier, perhaps) might tell you how some large orders are entered as one ice cream as it takes too long to enter them one by one. Or that Friday is busy, but the customers are primarily adults making quick decisions compared to children.

Discrepancies like these are common and can easily be spotted by domain experts.

Take into account unevenly distributed data

The AI model might suffer from low accuracy if data is unevenly distributed. For example, images of the faces of white people are more common than images of those with darker-coloured skin. This makes facial recognition less likely to recognise people of colour. Another example is predicting sales, where clients from some markets are rare, or some products are seldom bought.

There are several ways in which to handle this problem. One option is to not deal with rare labels and remove them from the training data. Our solution may still have a good business case without being able to handle the rare labels. Suppose you have a solution predicting delivery delays for transporting goods. You might not have many examples of certain types of deliveries, such as massive objects. You can remove these types of deliveries from the training data and not run a prediction for them.

Another option is to combine the rare labels into a larger category, covering more labels. Suppose you're making a document classifier. If some types of documents are so rare in a dataset that they only appear five or ten times compared to others 500-1,000 times, combining all rare document classes into a miscellaneous category can give a better user experience. If you choose to do this, remember to update your decision model, and get it cleared with stakeholders. This will reveal if the solution is viable.

A third option is to generate data synthetically as will be explained later in this chapter.

Noise

As mentioned above, I worked on a solution to predict whether a customer will accept an offer to buy a product. The AI model was based on historical offers and purchases. Imagine a customer acting irrationally, accepting a much higher price than usual. There can be many explanations for this, and you often have no chance to know why. That's noise. You can't know for sure what data is noise and what is a genuine signal, but all datasets almost certainly come with noise. With domain expert interviews and data cleaning, you can remove some noise as you understand the data better.

Environment

Ensure that the environment in which the training data is collected is the same or comparable to where the AI is used. That will improve the model's accuracy. For image models, say *object recognition models*, the environment is the surroundings of the object. The lighting, the angles, the background, and other conditions will affect the model's results. A classic mistake is to use images of products in a clean setting with a white background to train a model, hoping it will work in a store or warehouse. Imagine quality checks on an assembly line in a factory. If we collect images of assembly line objects in a clean setting, we will see the model becoming confused by the new background, resulting in lower accuracy.

When collecting data, try to imagine the different environments that might occur. Otherwise, ensure to align with stakeholders in an environment you know the AI will work. Stakeholders might not realise how much the effect of a new environment will have in terms of accuracy.

Closely related labels

Sometimes labels are closely related. That can happen for all data types. Images of Golden Retrievers might look like Labradors but not Rottweilers. Emails about purchases might look like product support emails, but not HR emails. Accounts on a chart of accounts for bookkeeping might be similar, like *purchase of goods* and *purchase of hardware* but not *rent*. In the case of closely related labels, you often want more data (records, such as lines in a spreadsheet) on these than other more distinguishable ones. It takes more examples for the algorithm to find the differences in this case confidently.

Closely related labels are not only more challenging for the machine to distinguish. Humans face the same challenges. That usually means two things. First, humans doing the data labelling are more likely to make mistakes, further hurting the accuracy. Second, agreeing on label definitions is more challenging than usual. If you see closely related labels, expect and plan for more work.

Hard to define labels

Clearly, defining the labels is a task in the data handling phase, as these definitions will persist through the model and affect the user experience.

The challenge is that we perceive and understand concepts differently. Suppose we are to define the labels "sold" and "not sold." It might seem obvious and indisputable whether a sale has occurred or not, but it is not. There are many steps in a sales process. An offer is made, an acceptance is given, and then the money and product are exchanged. Some might say the product is sold when the offer is accepted, and others when the payment is made.

And how do we deal with returns? If a product is returned, should we re-label it as "sold" as it's been sold once already or is it now "not sold"? It depends on the use case and how users expect the model to behave.

The solution is to agree on the label definitions in writing. Minor quirks will become apparent, and you might realise you're not as aligned as you thought.

Hitler-beetle rule for naming labels and features

Naming labels is also worth some consideration. When you name something, a label, or a feature, that name tends to stick and is impossible to change no matter how hard you try. As developers will code the name into database structures, API documentation and marketing material, it becomes impossible to change. I have often made the mistake of coming up with a name quickly, thinking I could change it later. I couldn't.

I call this the Hitler-Beetle rule referencing the Hitler Beetle bug (*anophthalmus hitleri* in Latin). The beetle was named after Adolf Hitler, at a time when that seemed appropriate. Several attempts have been made to change it, but it remains the same seventy years after the Second World War.

Names matter as they have connotations and meanings that affect how users and stakeholders perceive an item. Perform some sanity-checking of the names for labels or features.

DATA QUALITY

The quality of data determines the accuracy of your AI models. Data quality is often blamed as the reason for low model accuracy or why a specific solution will require a lot of data cleaning. But the term 'data quality' is broad and covers several categories of potential issues. Data can be unevenly distributed, insufficient, or faulty in many ways.

To make communicating and addressing data quality issues with stakeholders easier, here's a list of the issues you can experience. It's based on the mini data set on the house prices we briefly looked at in the beginning of the book.

Price	Postcode	Colour	m^2	Year built
€250k	2000	Yellow	190	1990
€140k	2200	Red	140	1960
€350k	2900	White	230	1930

Table 16: Data quality

Systematic missing records

Data often only covers a fraction of the potential historical records possible, which is no problem. We don't need images of all Labradors in history to make a Labrador recogniser, and we don't need all housing sales to predict prices. We can still achieve high-accuracy models with only a subset of all data.

The issue starts if the dataset, systematically, is missing labels. Perhaps a geographical area is missing in our housing price dataset, or we only have images of a particular family of Labradors.

The problem with systematically missing records is that we get unknown unknowns. This often results in models seemingly performing well when we're building them, but they underperform when used in production.

Wrong data points

We might see faults in the data points in a dataset. A square metre might have been entered incorrectly into the system. That kind of mistake is almost inevitable, but it isn't necessarily a problem if the errors are insignificant. With enough data (records), errors like that will have little to no impact on the model performance. The challenge with wrong data points is that they can be hard to spot. It often requires a domain expert to see that something is off.

Formatting issues

Sometimes data have different sources, or the collection method changes over time. Some housing sales data sources might write the same value in various formats. For the number of rooms in a house, that could be: "2", "2 rooms", "2 bedrooms", or "#2." That will have to be uniformed before being used for training.

Incorrect label values

There's also the possibility of mistakes in the label values (house price in this case). As with the data points, incorrect label values aren't a problem on a small scale.

Too few records

With too few records of housing sales, it won't be possible to achieve meaningful model accuracy.

Missing features

Features might be missing from a dataset. Features such as the number of rooms or square metres can cause performance issues, while features such as house colour might not be a problem.

Change of definitions or measurement

Definitions or measurements of labels or features can change over time, lowering the data quality. Suppose that square metres are altered to include a part of common areas in apartment buildings or that the price of a house includes a new tax or real estate fee. Changes like that happen frequently and are mostly outside our control.

USER-GENERATED DATA

Paperflow's competitors used invoice data entered by book-keepers to train their models. On the positive side, user-generated data is less costly than self-labelled data. On the negative side, you give up control over the data collection quality. Users don't have machine learning data in mind when working on their daily tasks.

A consideration is whether you can trust that users have the same objectives with the data as you. Imagine that the user is to select a payment date on an invoice. The payment date is written on the invoice. The user chooses the date by clicking its position in the invoice. But will the user always do that? Maybe they won't always pay on the invoice date. Perhaps the user agreed to something else with the supplier. Or the user can't afford to pay on the written payment day, so they type in another date.

That problem can occur in many different cases with data for AI. We will almost certainly lower the data quality by giving the user the task. The user seldom has the same sense of responsibility towards the data as required for AI. Even if the user wanted to, interpretation and lack of knowledge will distort the data.

HOW MUCH DATA AND AT WHAT COST?

Data collection can be a significant part of the cost of an AI solution. As a result, you need to know how much data is needed and the cost of collecting and cleaning it. There are several factors and choices that impact the amount of data, enabling you to adjust or get an indication of the cost.

BUILDING BLOCKS MATTER THE MOST FOR COLLECTION COSTS

When it comes to preparing data for an AI solution, some building blocks are almost cost-free, and some are expensive. The simplest and least costly building blocks are generally:

- image classification
- text classification
- sentiment analysis

For these building blocks, the data collection task is often only to sort the data into a folder of text or image files.

These building blocks are in the mid-range of costs:

- object detection
- intent analysis
- named entity recognition (NER)
- regression
- tabular classification (prediction)

Object detection, intent analysis, and NER require you to mark the data in a labelling tool. Regression and classification in tabular data can potentially be a single database query away and be ready for training. This is in the medium group, as the data structures often need insights from a developer working with it daily.

Cleaning and manipulation of data also vary in complexity. The following are demanding and expensive:

- image segmentation
- forecasting

Image segmentation requires precise marking around the objects. Forecasting tends to be costly data as time series have a more complex structure. This increases the need for data manipulation and preparation.

The jump in costs from one block to another can be huge. That's why you must consider if a feature request from a user or stakeholder requires a more expensive building block. If you're doing quality assurance on an assembly line, agreeing not just to spot damaged products but also to predict what part is damaged, can mean a tenfold increase in data costs. Make sure the business case also sees a similar increase in value if you accept a feature like that.

GENERATIVE AI DATA COSTS

Generative AI often requires no data at all as it's pre-trained. Instead, you may need to provide the AI access to documents, emails, or databases. Let's return to our AI sales rep. Here, it needs access to customer contracts, emails, and a product database. Getting access to data is cheaper than labelling large quantities of data, but there are still costs involved. A company's emails and contracts will have personal data or business-critical data that must be carefully assessed for relevance and potential data security. If we provide a generative AI solution full access to this data it will share all information, including the sensitive parts to users. As a result, we must go through all data and delete or mask the sensitive data before providing it with the solution. Alternatively, the solution has to have user-based access to each document, so we know that the user of the generative solution has the right to access all information of a given document. That is a costly setup to build as of now.

ADOPTION STRATEGIES AND DATA COSTS

The adoption strategies significantly impact the price of data. Off-the-shelf models are pre-trained and don't need training data.

Many companies do not believe they are ready to implement AI because they think their data is of poor quality and would therefore require a significant investment to get started. However, by using off-the-shelf or pre-trained generative AI, the investment in data is often low. Models like these are readily available:

Translation: AI translation comes in free, open-source, versions you can run locally or in Cloud API (pay-per-use) from providers such as Google and Microsoft.

Text similarity: Models that compare two texts are freely available from projects like Hugging Face. These can be implemented with a few lines of Python code and perform very well – at least in English. Text similarity can be used to compare documents, for example, when you want to find a contract from a library of contracts that looks like one you are working on.

Text-to-speech: Text-to-speech on cloud-based or open-source versions are also getting so good that it can provide helpful output in applications.

Speech-to-text: Speech-to-text can (in English, at least) write subtitles in movies and is today used for logging customer support calls that can later be used to analyse the conversation.

Text-to-image: Even creating an image from a line of text is getting impressively good. NVIDIAs solution, DALL-E 2, produces results that look human-made. Hugging Face also has an open-source version called DALL-E Mini.

For AutoAI solutions, you will often need surprisingly little data. That's mainly due to foundation models, but it's also because AutoAI algorithms are becoming so good at automatically finding the best model for the data provided.

FOUNDATION MODELS

Foundation models have been pre-trained with often millions of examples. A foundation model understands how basic features like shapes and colours interact with image data. For text and language, the foundation model already understands how language is structured.

LLMs are also foundation models, such as Google BERT (both an LLM and a foundation model) or GPT. Open-source vision foundation models can be used for vision building blocks. Using foundation models for tabular building blocks is possible, but this hasn't been popularised yet.

The training on top of foundation models is called *transfer learning,* as the learning transfers from the foundation model to the new model.

Foundation models can reduce the required amount of data by up to 95% to achieve the same model accuracy. That significantly impacts the business case, and looking for relevant foundation models is always a good idea.

Some foundation models are more specific. I recently worked with object detection in satellite images. It turns out that foundation models specifically trained on satellite images exist.

Foundation models are the driver behind the significant improvements in AI we see now.

THE DESIRED ACCURACY

Your accuracy goal is a factor with a significant impact on the cost of data. Remember how the decision modelling in the discovery phase made us set a goal for accuracy and how confident the model must be for us to implement a specific decision. Achieving higher accuracy requires more data. The added data and costs to the solution's development are subject to a classic diminishing return on investment relationship. The last few percentages are the hardest to achieve, and the cost associated with increasing accuracy from 90% to 92.5% can easily be the same as going from 80% to 90%. It's beneficial to clarify this to stakeholders and ensure expectations are calibrated. When project sponsors know the mechanics of costs and accuracy, they tend to have more realistic expectations.

OPTIMAL COST

There's a diminishing return of value on accuracy. That means increasing accuracy by two percentage points might not increase the business value by the same amount. That was the case with Paperflow.

Mistakes in book-keeping data are often caught later in the accounting process. As such, the difference in value between 98.5% correct and 99.5% accuracy is so tiny that the time spent fixing the mistakes would be hard to measure. On the other hand, the cost to achieve that accuracy increase could be huge. It would require collecting data from rare invoice layouts and precise data labelling, perhaps demanding a six-eye principle compared to the current four-eye principle, in turn increasing the labelling costs by 50%.

In line with classic business school logic, the optimal accuracy would be the highest difference between the cost of data and business value. Figure 8, which appears in chapter 8, is an excellent tool for communicating to stakeholders that higher accuracy isn't always a better business decision.

FASTER AND BETTER DATA LABELLING

Labelling can entail a significant cost, but there are methods you can use to save time and money.

MODEL-ASSISTED LABELLING

Model-assisted labelling is data collection where the people who label it (for example, marking an image as an image of a dog) are aided by suggestions from an AI model. Usually, a model is trained from the first batches of data labelled manually. That model can help suggest labels in future labelling tasks. AI will now pre-label the data, so people performing the labelling only must approve the labels in many cases. The model is constantly retrained as more data is labelled, improving the suggestions over time. The trained model can have the sole purpose of helping to label data faster, or it can be the model that will later be used in production. If you need to collect more data on an ongoing basis, the production model can be used. Many labelling tools now have built-in model-assisted labelling, so using this method isn't necessarily expensive.

Another advantage of model-assisted labelling is that you can see how the model performs for different labels early in the data handling phase instead of waiting until the model phase.

However, there are challenges with model-assisted labelling. People tend to be on autopilot when they do tedious work. The problem is that this means more mistakes. When using model-assisted labelling, the most prominent reason for mistakes is choosing an incorrect label the model has suggested. Humans tend to accept suggestions rather than challenge them. That bias hurts the accuracy of the assisting model. If the labelling by people keeps following increasingly worse suggestions, it lowers the quality of the data labelling.

You must also be careful not to enable model-assisted labelling too soon. It can be more time-consuming for data labellers to correct wrong suggestions than to have no suggestions.

ACTIVE LEARNING

Another way to make data collection more cost-effective is through *active learning*. This is a technique where the new data a model receives for prediction is subsequently sent for labelling in a prioritised order, based on the confidence score. The data that received the lowest confidence score are given the highest priority. In this way, one selects data for training where the model needs it most. This results in getting the most improved model quality for the same money.

For example, a model can recognise the difference between different dog breeds. In that case, some dog breeds will be challenging to distinguish from each other. In active learning, the data for further training is chosen by prioritising predictions with the highest uncertainties. The model might have the highest uncertainty on images of a Labrador or a Golden Retriever, as they look the most alike. When a prediction is made in production, the model will have a lower confidence score on these species than other more distinguishable species.

The image with the lowest confidence score is prioritised first for labelling. This can be set up to happen automatically.

A challenge with active learning is that you risk giving your model biases when providing the algorithm cherry-picked data for training.

Another consideration is whether teaching the model in the most challenging cases is necessarily the most important. The difference between Labradors and Golden Retrievers doesn't matter much regarding business value. Using active learning, you risk prioritising these labels all the time. The goal is still the user experience and business value; active learning doesn't consider that.

UNDERSTANDING AND ANALYSING DATA

After collecting and annotating data, you need to understand the data.

LOOK AT THE DATA

A famous example underlines the importance of looking at the data with a critical mind. The first example dates back to the Second World War. In England, a study was made of the bombers returning home from Germany, showing an obvious pattern in the bullet holes in the hull of the planes.[2] In the image, the bullet holes are clearly centred around the wing tips, the plane's centre, and the tail. The study revealed the importance of reinforcing these areas to make the aircraft more robust to being hit in these hotspots.

At least, that was the initial idea. Luckily an engineer realised a more truthful story from this data. He realised that the planes shot in other areas and never made it home to England should be a part of this dataset. The lack of planes returning with bullet holes in the engines and the front must have meant that the aircraft that got hit in these areas crashed. Thus, the areas without bullets were the important ones to reinforce.

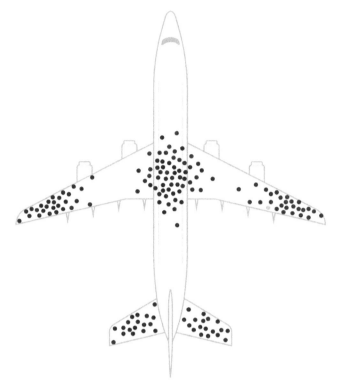

Figure 12: Looking at data critically

Similarly, the sales data in SundAI didn't tell us how many ice creams we could have sold as a too-long queue at the store would deter potential customers. These potential sales were like the crashed fighter planes, nowhere to be found in the data.

A case like this also underlines the value of collecting no results — the data for when we're unsuccessful. The British engineers must have had a clear idea of how many planes made it home and how many didn't. Many companies only log the data with a positive outcome, making it hard to make predictions.

I recently worked with a hotel chain on predicting conference bookings. The hotels habitually logged calls from potential clients inquiring about conference facilities. That data was precious as it gave an idea about lost revenue on the already fully booked days. It significantly affects the business case if the potential for bookings is 10% or five times higher than capacity on the most attractive days.

BLACK SWANS

Another noteworthy concept in understanding your data is the *Black Swan* theory. The name was coined by statistician and author of *Fooled by Randomness*, Nassim Nicholas Taleb.[3]

For many years it was common wisdom that black swans didn't exist. As they'd never been observed, they didn't exist in any record. Had you, back then, to put a bet on the colour of the next swan you saw, you would probably not bet on black. No black swans had ever been seen, so the chance of the next one would be 0%, right?

It turned out that there were lots of black swans. They just hadn't been observed yet. It first happened when we discovered Australia, which was full of black swans. In other words, the data only represented the known and observed world, not the actual world. That's a core challenge when working with data. Our data shows us the observable world, while the task is to represent the actual world.

Black swans are, on an individual level, very rare. The recent COVID-19 pandemic was a testament to a rare black swan event. The financial crisis in 2007 was similar. Historically, the housing market had never crashed, so any model built on historical data couldn't have predicted such an event. But black swans aren't rare on an aggregated level. They're more common than you would intuitively think. Pandemics, crashing housing markets or war in Europe seem like such unique events that they must be uncommon, but less media-attractive rare events happen all the time.

Whatever your data shows from historical events is just history – the future can be vastly different. That also translates to the accuracy of models. As AI models use parts of historical training data to calculate their accuracy, they do so based on how they would have performed in the past. Always expect AI models to perform at least a bit worse in production than the model accuracy measurements tell us.

Don't try to predict black swans – by nature, they're unpredictable. Instead, ensure that your business processes can handle black swans. When you build your decision models, remember that the model can provide a high confidence score and be wrong at any time. It can happen once in a blue moon or start happening consistently from a particular point in time. COVID-19 was a black swan that resulted in many forecasts and predictions being confident but wrong from one day to the next.

Ensure you have a plan ready for operating without the predictions from your AI solution for a while if an event like COVID-19 happens. For one-time events, you should be able to either absorb the cost or handle the mistake. If your AI solution is a fraud-detection model that confidently predicts *not-fraud* costing you much money as a one-off, that hopefully is outweighed by the gain from the caught fraudsters. But how about a self-driving car that crashes in a black swan event? Well, that's where the airbags become relevant. In business processes relying on AI, we can either absorb the cost or invest in airbags.

DATA BIAS

Bias is a term you can't avoid when working with AI. AI or algorithmic bias is the idea of systematic skewing in either the data or the model. The result is that the predictions by the model also become systemically skewed, often negatively impacting the business case. An example could be that most images of dogs are surrounded by green grass in a garden. A model might be inclined to guess dog over cat if an image of a cat in the grass is presented.

Bias has a negative connotation in the media as it can result in the models performing in a way that favours some groups while disfavouring others. Examples include image generation models, producing a dark-skinned person when prompted with the word "criminal" and a light-skinned person when prompted with "CEO."

Bias is a reality and something we need to take seriously. However, in a business context, it is not limited to situations where groups of people are favoured or disfavoured. Bias is the term we use for any failure in an AI model's prediction caused by systematic distortion in the data.

There's also a bias around biases. The result of bias is that the model's prediction doesn't reflect the real world. But here's the catch. There is no single real or true world. The book-keepers from Paperflow disagreed on how to understand an invoice. You might also have tried reflecting on an event with others present. You may attend the same event and have two entirely different experiences. That's bias. Bias exists in everything, and completely avoiding bias isn't possible. When you build AI solutions, expect bias.

MITIGATING BIAS

Data bias

If the bias originates in the data, it must be fixed there. Data collection is significantly exposed to the risk of systemic flaws.

There are two main reasons: the observed world from where we collect data already has bias making our input skewed.

Racial biases are a good example from the observed world. In some parts of the world, people with dark-coloured skin are judged more harshly and pulled over more often in traffic. The data will reflect that. To avoid bias like this, you need to manipulate the data to no longer reflect it. For example, some neighbourhoods are dominated by certain ethnicities. A postcode feature could therefore reveal this information. Removing that feature will exclude the information from training data. In cases like that, AI solutions can lower bias and provide a fairer treatment of people.

Bias occurs when we don't collect training data randomly and representatively. As some data might be easier to gather systematically, it will affect data collection. For example, collecting data on certain income levels might be easier. Collecting data by scraping the internet or doing online surveys through social media might also be tempting. But people who use online platforms or spend time online are probably not a fair representation of people in general.

You can spot bias risks if you know the problem and involve domain experts. Doing this early in the process makes enquiring about your suspicion of bias easy. If you build AI to predict whether customers will accept your offer, bias can come from how sales are logged. Some customers might be handled differently, or some sales departments or sales might have specific habits that skew the data.

Model bias

Bias can also be introduced when building the model and amplify already existing bias in the data. From a business perspective, it's enough to know that this is a risk, and that even with well-balanced data, the models might have significant bias. Bias in models can be both measured and monitored to an extent. For example, the accuracy of different groups represented via features or labels can be monitored to keep track of bias.

Bias can also increase over time if a feedback loop gets data in a systematically skewed way. That's especially a risk as the predictions made by the AI affect the decisions made by users, which can be understood from the debate on police and racial profiling. Suppose the police aim to optimise their efforts by targeting people most likely to be charged at a "random" traffic stop. If a group of people of a specific race are slightly more likely to be charged at a traffic stop, stopping more people from that group will be more efficient for the police. As charges result in fines – or even prison – the social problems that follow over time make it even more effective to focus on that group. That data feeds back into statistics, and the police seeking to be more efficient will target that group even more. AI solutions can introduce the same problem at a much higher scale, due to the speed at which we can make predictions and retrain the models.

DATA AS A COMPETITIVE ADVANTAGE

For companies that build AI products that compete on accuracy, data provides a competitive advantage. That was our situation at Paperflow. There are always limited resources, and you must choose between putting your efforts into collecting more or better data or building more advanced or higher-quality models. Always go for the data option. Data is the main competitive advantage you can give yourself in AI, especially if you're building something that competes with similar solutions. An AutoAI model made in three hours by a super user can beat that of a top data scientist building handcrafted models if the data is marginally better.

As AI has become easier to build the playing field is levelled as far as the modelling is concerned, data will have a higher level of importance in terms of success. Collecting data faster, in a higher quality or cheaper will provide you with training data that will enable you to beat your competitors.

Companies working with AI underestimate this effect, because operationalising and optimising data collection is nowhere near as exciting and sexy as model development and machine learning. Management and the business side have no clue how to prioritise, and the data science team will be biased towards improving models instead of data. Although data collection is the tedious side of AI, it's the winning horse from a business perspective.

PERSONAL DATA

Personal data or *personally identifiable information* (PII) is often unavoidable in AI. It comes with challenges and limitations that you need to handle.

PII is any data that can be referred to a specific person, such as their name, address, or phone number. Data containing PII must be handled with more care – sometimes it's best to avoid it completely. Data containing PII is subject to regulation in many parts of the world, such as the EU's General Data Protection Regulation (GDPR). If identifiable data is paired with information on sensitive matters such as health or political interests, the degree of regulation and amount of caution needed increases.

PII doesn't need to be a concrete reference to a specific person; it's anything that could identify a person. That could be a picture where someone is recognisable or a story where names and references are removed but still can be used to identify someone.

CHALLENGES

Ethics and regulations around PII bring a set of challenges. First, collecting and processing PII data might require consent from the people to whom the data refers, depending on local legislation and organisation policies. Sometimes not only a general consent, but consent to acquire it for each individual use case is required. You must get user consent if PII is obtained for an AI solution predicting churn. If you'd later like to use the same data to optimise prices, you need consent for that as well. When PII requires consent depends on local laws and regulations.

The second challenge is that regulations such as GDPR is interpreted differently for each country and organisation. What might be acceptable use in one company might be a no-go in another. Two similar organisations in the same market can have legal departments with different perceptions and procedures.

Storing data containing PII requires added security, such as encryption, and sometimes limitations on where you can store it. Many public and private organisations in Europe will not store PII in a public cloud, such as AWS, Google Cloud or Microsoft Azure. When that's the case, many of the built-in AI solutions in the cloud are no longer available, which can quickly increase project costs.

Finally, PII often limits how long you can store data – I've seen limitations as little as two weeks. Training AI models at a decent accuracy on data that only covers the last two weeks is often not feasible.

HANDLING PII

Handling PII when building AI solutions can induce higher costs, but some initiatives can mitigate this.

Contact your legal department when initiating a new AI solution as soon as possible. Legal can spend months figuring out what they can and can't allow. If you do this too late, the entire project can be put on hold. Try to initiate the legal discussion in pre-analysis or early in the discovery phase.

Also, consider if you really need the data that contains PII. Suppose you're building an AI solution recommending products to users. In that case, you might instinctively think that gender, income, or location information on a potential customer will significantly improve the model's accuracy. But basing your models on other factors such as the current behaviour, that does not include PII – say, what product the customer is showing interest in now – can be sufficient.

You can also deploy and run AI solutions where it's possible to get data access with fewer legal requirements. Suppose you're doing object detection on people. In that case, you can deploy and run the AI solution on a computer at the camera position, so you don't have to transfer PII images to a server or cloud. You can also run models on local machines or data centres. It usually requires more engineering work but can save you much trouble. Synthetic data is also a brilliant solution for replacing data containing PII.

Handling PII issues doesn't have to be a costly or limiting factor for applying AI. In fact, finding innovative ways to lower the need for PII while keeping accuracy high or using more secure methods for handling PII can be a strategic advantage. If for example you're building AI solutions that compete with other AI solutions, having fewer PII issues can be a great marketing and sales pitch with which to win new customers.

SYNTHETIC DATA

Synthetic data is fabricated by humans or algorithms, not actual world observations. Just like real data, they are used to represent the world in which the AI is supposed to function. A simple example of synthetic data is a customer review. Imagine we want to create an AI that can convert written customer feedback into a score from 1 to 10, where 1 is a very frustrated, and 10 is a perfectly happy customer. If we don't have access to real feedback or only have very few responses, we can write our own or get, for example, ChatGPT to write them. For instance, we could write, 'I will never shop with you again' and give it a score of 2, and write, 'Fantastic experience' and give it a score of 8. Whether 8 and 2 are correct scores, we can't know for sure, but if we have seen a lot of feedback ourselves or have shown many reviews to ChatGPT, then we can reproduce reviews with reasonable accuracy. By doing this on a large scale, we can create enough data to train a classification model that automatically gives a score. We can choose to train on the synthetic data alone or mix it with real data.

Synthetic data has several possible purposes:

ADD DATA TO LABELS WITH NO OR LITTLE DATA

If our store in the previous example never or only rarely received scores of 1 or 2, our review model would not be able to predict these scores. Here, we can instead fill in with synthetic data and develop our own reviews. This is also helpful if you have a 'skewed' dataset as explained at the beginning of the chapter.

REMOVE PERSONAL DATA

If our reviews contain personal data, we can create synthetic versions that do not. This can include specific data such as names and addresses, but also if the texts contain stories about customers that are so unique, they become personally identifiable.

An example could be a review text like, 'My shipment to address X got lost!' By showing enough examples like this to a language model, it can write reviews about lost shipments and invent fictional addresses.

WHETHER DATA IS SYNTHETIC DEPENDS ON THE USE

The line between what is synthetic data and what is not can seem hard to understand. When I say that reviews written by ChatGPT are synthetic data, does that mean that all data coming from an AI solution is synthetic?

No, whether it is or not depends on the use. If we use the output to mimic the real data we know, then it is synthetic data. Everything else is real data. The difference is whether we observe data and see it as its 'own truth' or create it to resemble another truth. This means that the same data for one person can be synthetic and real for another. A bit confusing, like everything else in AI.

SYNTHETIC DATA WILL BECOME A BIG DEAL

Since synthesising can add data where we lack it and replace personal data where we need to, it has a lot of potential. It can improve privacy, reduce bias, and increase model accuracy. Therefore, I am convinced that most data in the future for AI will be entirely or partially synthetic. In fact, Gartner, the American consulting firm researching technology, already said in 2021 that, 'By 2024, 60% of the data used for the development of AI and analytics projects will be synthetically generated.'[4] Whether this turns out to be true so quickly, we will soon see.

TYPES OF SYNTHETIC DATA

Depending on the data type (text, images and tabular data), different techniques exist for creating synthetic data and use cases.

SYNTHETIC TEXTS

With language models like ChatGPT, you can generate synthetic texts that resemble human-written texts, just as in the example above.

In my company, we used this approach for an email classification case where real data could only be stored for three months due to PII. The short time made it hard to keep up with seasonal-specific signals. We fed the real emails a language model and fine-tuned the model to produce synthetic emails. We could then generate unlimited data for each label to train the AI models without personal data. The accuracy was high, and the synthetic data could be kept forever.

SYNTHETIC IMAGES

With text-to-image models like Stable Diffusion, we can create synthetic image data. The images can be used for training data, art, inspiration, and online content.

The most well-known of these are DALL-E, Stable Diffusion, and Midjourney, which can produce realistic images. You can prompt the model with a short text telling it what images to create. The prompt can be, "apple on a kitchen table", or, "blue strawberry in an expressionistic style."

Figure 13: Synthetic image data

These images are produced in seconds and can be made in large amounts quickly, effectively providing unlimited images.

Text-to-image models are trained on millions of images found on the internet, and using images produced for text-to-image models as synthetic data has many use cases. For example, you can produce images of objects you'd like to classify with AI. You may want images of different types of fruits to make a fruit classifier. You can also use it to augment images you already have. For example, you can make versions of images of people with different skin colours. That way, you can remove some of the bias issues discussed above. You can also use it to make new random or pre-defined backgrounds for objects. With that, you can fix the assembly line environment problem discussed earlier.

There are challenges with text-to-image models. At the time of writing, the first lawsuits on intellectual property are being filed against the model providers. The question is do the models infringe the IP rights of the image owners on whom the models are trained. The jury is still out on this issue, so relying too heavily on image-to-text models comes with some risk.

Another challenge is that these models also have a bias. I already mentioned that they would render images with lighter skin colour when prompting for a CEO and darker if prompting for a criminal. If you choose to use AI-rendered images for training data, be aware that it's likely to be biassed.

SYNTHETIC TABULAR DATA

It is also possible to create synthetic tabular data. This is done by first training a model on real existing data, which can then 'predict' new synthetic tabular data.

The records have the "same distribution," meaning that the synthetic data has the same statistical distribution – or pattern of values – as the original data. It allows the synthetic data to preserve the relationships between features and labels that exist in the original data.

A common use case for synthetic tabular data is to expand existing datasets with more records. That could be housing prices above or below a specific price range. It can also make data anonymous, as synthetically generated records can't be traced back to specific individuals. Healthcare is currently a sector at the forefront of using synthetic tabular data, as record privacy is taken very seriously. This is due to the need to share data between hospitals and research groups. By synthetically generating health data based on real cases, the patterns are preserved and can be used to train AI models for research and diagnostics. Any case with limited access to tabular data due to privacy might be a good case.

The challenge of synthetic tabular data is like the other types: bias can be amplified when synthesising it.

MODELS OF THE WORLD

With synthetic models, we can, at a fraction of the cost, experiment with AI solutions before releasing them and teaching them for improvement. Self-driving cars are a perfect use case for this. They can be developed faster and safer by building a synthetic model of the world close to reality, modelling with real-world physics and random scenarios. Most companies making self-driving cars use models built in the Unity engine, initially intended for computer game development. Cars can drive, crash, and improve millions of times without humans at risk in a virtual world before release.

Computer models that simulate the world have been around for a long time. The new thing is that they are generated automatically, making building large and realistic models affordable.

SUMMARY

The data handling phase is an explorative exercise in finding ways to collect the needed data in the required amounts in the most efficient way. If you're smart about collecting data, you can turn it into a competitive advantage.

You also need to understand and explore the data you have. That can be tricky as data is a tricky storyteller, and you must often refer back to domain experts to understand it.

The future holds less need for data acquisition due to the foundation models and synthetically generated data. Even so, the tools and practices mentioned here will be relevant for years to come.

CHAPTER 10
DEVELOPING AI

In this phase, we have two main objectives:

1. training models to the needed accuracy while understanding how they perform
2. making models available at the scale and speed necessary for the use case

Training models entails exploring different algorithms and modelling approaches to provide the best accuracy with the available data. The second objective, making models available, is done by building the infrastructure for hosting, maintaining, and sometimes retraining the models.

This last step of operations covers the monitoring phase of the method, which is chronologically after the implementation phase but is so strongly connected to the development phase that it makes more sense to explain it here.

THE DEVELOPMENT PHASE ACTIVITIES

The activities of the development phase are:

- training the models
- understanding the models
- building retraining flows
- integrating with other systems
- setting up monitoring of models

TEAM ROLES IN AI PROJECTS AND THEIR CHALLENGES

Different technical team roles in an AI team have different responsibilities for the various components. You usually need data science, data engineering, software development and DevOps (IT infrastructure) skills to build AI solutions. That brings challenges.

Data scientists or machine learning engineers who build models often only have shallow skills in areas other than their own. That makes AI teams more complicated to handle from a business perspective, as more specialists are often needed than for traditional software solutions. In conventional software development, you usually have teams consisting of front-end and back-end developers. Depending on the chosen adoption strategy, data scientists, data engineers and even ML Ops specialists might be necessary on top of the software developers for AI.

The spread of competencies is a significant challenge in AI. A team of four building an AI product can consist of a front-end developer, a back-end developer, a data engineer, and data scientists. That composition makes an AI team much more vulnerable than a traditional development team that, also with four people, could consist of two back-end developers and two front-end developers. With more specialists required, you're more vulnerable to setbacks if a team member catches a cold or leaves. In IT, we use the "bus factor", referring to how many people on the team can be hit by a bus tomorrow without seriously hurting the progress of a project. In AI, the bus factor is often half that in traditional software development.

We struggled with exactly that challenge in Paperflow. I had no previous experience in AI, so I was blindsided. Even as our team grew, the dependency on individual people was higher than usual. Not only was it a business risk, but it was also a stressful experience for the employees. Knowing you're the only one who can solve a specific problem that others depend on or the only one who can fix a bug in a system is stressful.

One solution to lower the dependency on too many different skills is to use as much pre-developed AI infrastructure as possible from cloud providers. That could be a managed database, API endpoints, pre-built retraining flows or AutoAI.

Another solution is to take on an external contractor for a while. If you're in a large organisation, you can do that internally. The software development tasks of building integrations to other IT systems and building the user interface can be done by externals. Data science and data engineering are usually the best elements to keep on the team.

If I were tasked with building Paperflow all over again, the team risk would be enough for me to implement more AutoAI and rely more on available cloud infrastructure.

STILL A NEED FOR DATA SCIENTISTS?

For applying generative models such as ChatGPT, you might ask if employing data scientists is even necessary as all the modelling and data have been done already. You integrate with a simple API, provide it a prompt, and get a response. Couldn't anyone build their own AI support-answer solution if that is the case?

First – yes, but it still makes sense to employ a data scientist. Under-standing the model's behaviour, adding the right tools and utilising the possibilities of the LLMs are still very much a data scientist game. However, many solutions can be built by non-data scientists, just like you can build your own website with services such as Wix or Squarespace. Note that introducing such tools hasn't meant a decrease in demand for web developers.

ANATOMY OF AI SOLUTIONS

The typical AI solution consists of the following components:

- model(s)
- prediction pipeline
- data storage or connection
- retraining flow
- front-end (user interface)
- integrations

To bind these components together, we often write *glue code*, a traditional software development code that can be a substantial part of an AI solution. A famous Google research paper (Hidden Technical Debt in Machine Learning Systems) looked at many AI solutions and concluded that 95% of code in AI solutions is glue code.[1] For that reason, building AI still includes the substantial task of traditional software development. Many AI projects have failed by underestimating the size and the importance of the glue code.

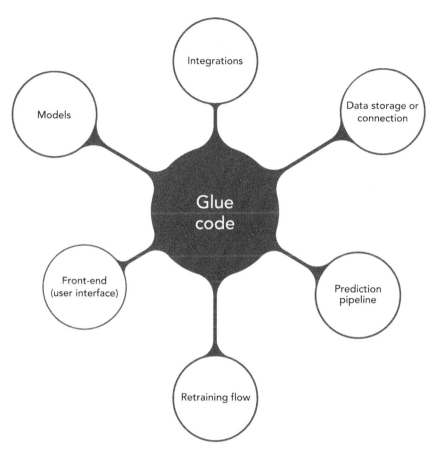

Figure 14: Anatomy of AI solutions

Imagine you're building the forecasting solution for SundAI. You might want to extract data from the ERP, the shift-planner system, and weather reports. You then want to store that data, clean and manipulate it, so it fits the structure that makes it possible to either retrain or query your models for predictions. You need to serve these predictions to another system via API integration or an application front-end. These components require a traditional software development approach.

MODEL(S) AND PREDICTION PIPELINE

Figure 15: Prediction model

The prediction model (in this SundAI case, the forecasting model) is the centre of the AI solution. But to make predictions, we need data from the ERP (last week's sales) and data from the weather forecast. Getting that data is known as a *prediction pipeline*. In this pipeline, we need to:

- fetch query data from the data source
- manipulate the data from the source format to the format used by the model
- store the data
- predict based on the given data
- store or send the prediction results to other services

Data engineers or traditional software developers traditionally build this pipeline in larger teams, while it's often been made the data scientists' responsibility in smaller teams, although they mostly have little training or experience in this area.

Retraining flow

A retraining flow is an automated pipeline that collects labelled data from a storage or source. It then manipulates it to be used to train or update a new model based on the same structure as an existing one. The retraining is initiated automatically or based on factors such as model performance, available training data, or time.

A retraining flow isn't a mandatory component. Many AI solutions are built and shipped without retraining, as none is needed. The object recognition that classifies tree species might be trained once and deployed without ever being retrained. In other cases, like the forecasting model at SundAI, you might want to build a retraining flow. The need for retraining depends on the drift.

A common misconception is that retraining comes as a default in AI solutions. It's far from this. In fact, the retraining flow is often the most time-consuming and challenging part to build. Retraining means acquiring data, cleaning it, storing data, training a model, ensuring its accuracy is good, and maybe even checking for bias and other risks after each iteration. Building an AI solution can be two to three times more expensive than a similar solution without retraining if that's to be done.

Monitoring

A monitoring component is a tool that measures and presents the model's performance. As mentioned above, the accuracy will eventually decrease due to drift. Countless pre-made tools and frameworks can monitor accuracy.

Performance in querying time can also be necessary to monitor. Querying a model to make a prediction can take as little as a few milliseconds. If you're querying the model thousands of times per minute, scaling computing power might be necessary to keep the prediction speed high. For some systems, like SundAI's forecasting, a few extra seconds of response time have no effect. For others, like a search engine, the added seconds can ruin the user experience and hurt the overall business case.

Interface

The interface component is the user interface (front-end) or API (technical integration), enabling users or other systems to interact with the AI solution.

The interface is a crucial component, whether API or front-end, as the interaction provides the data features used in the prediction. It's also where the user or other IT see the results of the AI predictions. If the interface is misunderstood or there are issues in the input or output part, the solution's value is lower. That's also why I stressed the efforts in UX work in the discovery phase. But the same effort must be put into the interface if it's an API. A reliable and understandable *documented* API is necessary for correct use.

GENERATIVE MODELS

Generative models come pre-trained and can be fine-tuned for your purpose. For LLMs, that means providing texts (for example, emails) from which you want it to learn. Although fine-tuning takes way less computing power than training the full model, it can still be a large task.

Part of this process could be incorporating terminology specific to a particular field, for example, legal or medical terms.

Hallucinations

Sometimes generative AI models will output wrong content, often in a confident manner. As an example, you might ask ChatGPT to list the top five books of a specific author and chances are that you will get back five books even if the author has only written three. The last two are just made up. It seems to be impossible to totally avoid hallucinations is generative AI, though the vendors producing the models are working hard to lower the risks.

Guardrails

Guardrails for generative solutions mean limiting the output's range of possible outcomes. This is especially done to avoid hallucinations, undesirable behaviour, such as discrimination, or limiting the user's options in the solution. For example, let's say you're building an AI agent to answer support emails for a product. Here, we would prefer the agent to only invent solutions to the customer's problems that are feasible with the product. In this case, one can guardrail the agent to only find solutions based on the product's documentation or previous support email responses. We can also set limitations on which questions an agent should answer. For example, all questions about prices or competing products can be referred to sales, even though the LLM has enough data to answer the question. Notice that with the current state of the technology, guardrails are not guaranteed to work perfectly as uncertainty is a fundamental feature of AI.

There are several ways in which you can implement guardrails:

- Fine tuning the LLM
- Prompt-engineering
- Limiting the output format (Like HTML or XML)
- Adjusting the temperature.

Temperature

Many generative algorithms include a user-controllable parameter called *temperature*. A low-temperature setting produces outcomes very similar to each other, given the same input, while a high-temperature setting produces dissimilar outcomes. You can set a high temperature for increased diversity and reduce it when focusing on a particular area in the output space.

Here's an example: Imagine you have a generative model designed to create digital artwork based on a theme, such as, "forest landscapes." When you use this model, you can adjust the temperature parameter to control the diversity of the outcomes.

Low-Temperature Setting: If you set the temperature to a low value the model will generate a series of very similar images in style, composition and content. Each image will likely feature the same elements, such as trees, a river, and perhaps animals. This setting is useful when you want to explore slight variations of a specific idea or scope.

High-Temperature Setting: Now, if you increase the temperature setting, the same input, will result in a much wider variety of outcomes. One image might depict a dense, tropical rainforest with vibrant colours, another might show a snowy forest with a stark, monochrome palette, and yet another could present a surreal, fantastical forest with imaginative elements like floating trees. High-temperature setting is ideal when you haven't settled on a specific scope or idea and want to explore possibilities.

Temperature settings can be used in any generative model and could as well have been texts that are generated for email campaigns, documentation or even code. In all scenarios it gives you the opportunity to fine tune what you have or to stay explorative.

MINDSET FOR BUILDING AI

Having the right approach and mindset when building models is crucial when applying AI. The right approach is to build a good enough solution fast, and the right mindset focuses on business outcomes.

Remember, the AI model is 5% to 10% of the solution, and as a result, successful implementation requires attention to the other 90% or 95%. That also means how you experiment with the solution and its user interface, during development, planning, and testing with users. No single part of the product can make it a success. It's an interacting system that can only win in it's entirety but fail due to a single element.

In the development phase, it's essential to bring that mindset to the table and focus not on the model accuracy or the interface's colours, but on the business outcome you've set to meet.

EXPERIMENT EFFICIENTLY

AI is experimental at its core. Therefore, an experimental approach is also required in the development phase. Finding suitable algorithms and models to get the highest possible accuracy is (even for a proficient data scientist) often a process of trial and error.

It's easy to get lost and experiment for too long to make a tiny increase in model accuracy with little business impact. It feels great every time you squeeze a little extra accuracy out of the model. Professional pride also often drives data scientists to aim for the most advanced technology or best performance in models.

If you're responsible for a data science team, it's your job to limit experimentation to an optimal level that's often lower than what specialists prefer. They mostly feel that it's possible to do more. They also feel responsible for the result—especially the ambitious ones. It's also easy to forget when experimenting that a novel modelling technique is more costly to maintain than an older, more proven one.

It's your role to remind the team of the bigger picture and show how the other components in the solution, user experience, trust and reliability also matter. That not all efforts can be used in modelling. You must remind the team that the users will judge the solution based on their experience with it, not its accuracy.

END-TO-END FIRST

When building an AI solution, you should build an end-to-end system as early as possible. That means a system that includes an entire prediction pipeline from data sources to delivering predictions. Imagine SundAI's forecasting model. It needs data from weather services and ERP, and we need to provide the results into a dashboard or maybe back into the ERP. Building this flow is a higher priority than building the AI model.

Figure 16: End to end first

The initial model could be a forecast that outputs the same numbers as last year, with an added growth factor of +5% - no more advanced than that. You can build and deploy more advanced models after the end-to-end flow prototype has been completed.

Building this flow first might be counterintuitive, as a well-performing model is the ultimate goal, but it will pay off. When you make the flow, many small surprises will appear. Sometimes data from a system like the SundAI ERP won't be as accessible as first promised. It might need more manipulation, or you might get more data features than expected, which can be used for a better model. There's also a chance that a third party, maybe a system vendor, needs to be involved in making software updates and amending code for the solution to work.

Going end-to-end is also in line with making the decision model before the prediction model. It clears the way early for potential problems before you've spent too much effort modelling. Suppose the ERP vendor needs to update the code. You might have to postpone the project deadline for another month. As time is a leading risk factor, you've added more risk. Going end-to-end first lowers risk.

BE READY TO START OVER WITHIN TWENTY-FOUR HOURS

An essential aspect of a productive mindset in the development phase is to be ready to scrap what you've built and start over. The first idea to solve a problem is probably not the best, and the same goes for model building. Whether you're the model builder or an AI building team manager, be willing to start over and seek out new approaches if the current one doesn't perform well.

In Paperflow, we often stuck with ideas for too long, trying to increase performance from a dead-end idea. We often believed that a significant improvement would happen with a bit more time and effort – it didn't. Hours became days, days became weeks and soon months. In AI, you must produce a high-quality result within a short time or abandon the strategy. This is the *24-rule*. If you can't produce satisfying results within twenty-four hours of work, given that your data is somewhat prepared when building models, the strategy is most likely not the right one. Cut your losses early, even if it hurts to tell developers or stakeholders that a new approach is necessary. In a business setting, you're rarely in a position where you can keep betting on a far-fetched experiment that might end up with a genius algorithm. Leave that to researchers. You can always return to an abandoned strategy if conditions or insight changes and makes it viable.

If you hit the wall on the 24-hour rule, your problem might be elsewhere than the model building, especially if it happens several times

Given that you have the needed competencies for model building, the issue is most likely in either the data quality, data features available, or the definition of the problem. In this case, consider going back and revisiting previous phases or abandoning the solution.

SPEED IS OF THE ESSENCE

Much research into project management points to a single factor that can affect the success or failure. That factor is time. As soon as you start a project, time is of the essence. The longer the project, the more significant the risk of failure. This rule applies to everything from building bridges to organisational change, software development, and AI.

The reason is that elements like stakeholders, sub-vendors, politics and finances change. With more time comes more change. A new manager can join a company and change priorities. A supplier can go bust, or your company's finances can change. AI has many moving parts, especially with data and technology. The data features impacting the model can also change. If you're too slow, you can risk new features being introduced, meaning that you need other data sources or new models. And the technology changes fast in AI, making it attractive to change technological parts of the solution during development if it takes too long.

There's also the softer side – the motivation of project stakeholders. The users, domain experts, and others won't have the same motivation and excitement forever.

Once you understand the problem and have the data, build fast. Allocate the resources needed to complete the phase fast rather than spreading the project for longer.

SIMPLEST APPROACH POSSIBLE

When building the AI solution (especially the first version), strive for the simplest approach possible. That means the one with the simplest algorithm, the fewest data features, the fewest labels, and the most proven technology.

The simplest approach aligns with the focus on business outcomes rather than technology. You may be surprised how often a low-effort solution quickly will solve the problem or provide valuable insight into what does and doesn't work. Again, it's easy to lock in on new promising technology, and the urge to work with exciting new solutions is always there. But that's better suited for a later version of a solution.

The idea is like the *minimal viable product* (MVP) or even the *minimum loveable product* (MLP) idea, but it's not the same. You might call it the *minimal effort product,* as you're trying to minimise the tech effort while preserving the objective of the business case.

AutoAI is always worth testing. If it fixes the problem or part of the problem, that might save valuable time. You can always go for a more complicated solution if it doesn't work.

Another simple approach to building AI is to select fewer data features. You might have identified several features in the discovery phase that you expect to be necessary to make correct predictions. At this stage, you only have expectations of the effect of the features, but no final truth. Some features for SundAI, such as information about nearby events, could require a lot of effort to acquire. Start by building with easy-to-attain features only, even when domain experts say performance will be low.

The easiest solution is often the best for all parties. It's easy to maintain and update, and it's usually also the one with the best performance.

At the same time, as AI technology improves, the chance of the lazy approach working fine gets higher and higher.

BUILDING AND UNDERSTANDING MODELS

Building models is done by applying and tweaking algorithms to the available dataset. That's a technical task. If you do not have a technical role in the project, you just need to understand the relationship between building blocks, models, algorithms, and data. You should know most of that by now, but let's recap the model definition.

A model is a program representing how the algorithm interprets the training data. The program can predict new data as that representation is applied. The task now is understanding how the models perform. That requires understanding how to measure accuracy and how that translates into practical business relevance.

UNDERSTANDING MODELS

Once a model has been trained, you need to understand two things.

- how accurate the model is
- the reasoning or mechanics behind model predictions

The latter is referred to as *explainable AI*.

Model accuracy

Model accuracy refers to how often it makes a correct prediction. There are different ways to calculate statistical and perceive accuracy versus business value.

A "95% accurate" model doesn't mean you can achieve 95% of the potential business value. Accuracy must be understood and inter-preted for each AI solution, considering business context, data quality, and model type.

It's also not necessarily good or bad to be 95% correct. I'm sometimes asked, for example, if 83% is a reasonable accuracy. 5% would be fantastic if the task were to guess the winning lottery numbers. That would make you a millionaire in no time. On the other hand, 95% isn't useful for a self-driving car that reads traffic lights.

If you have limited data due to funding or technical limits, an other-wise low accuracy could be decent if you consider limitations and low costs.

Model accuracy from a model perspective

Models measure their own accuracy. That's why accuracy doesn't mean real-world accuracy, but the model's perception of accuracy, given the data provided. When AI models are trained, the data is split into three sets.

- The *training set* is the data the algorithm uses to build the model.
- The *validation set* is the data used to optimise the model after training.
- The *test set* is the data used to test the model's accuracy. The test set isn't shown to the algorithm during training and, as a result, can be used to test prediction accuracy.

The split between training, test and validation is normally undertaken at an 80/10/10 ratio. it can also be done randomly; in some situations, the split is done based on other factors. For forecasting, the test and validation can be the "newest" data to make the performance measure more contemporary. That means explaining the accuracy to users must be done carefully – 99% model accuracy can easily translate to 90% experienced by users.

When you train new and better-performing models and deploy them instead of existing ones, the model's accuracy is seldom exactly comparable. New data features or algorithm changes can drastically change model accuracy without significantly changing real-world accuracy. As that change often happens in early-stage development, spending too much time on accuracy at this stage is not helpful.

Accuracy, recall and precision

There are different ways in which to calculate overall accuracy. Three of the most important are accuracy, recall and precision. Notice that the term *accuracy* is both used as a general term covering all kinds of accuracy measurements, but also a specific way to measure as will be described below. You can use the measurements to optimise models for different use cases to better explain accuracy. It can also be helpful to present accuracy to users in a way that better reflects their experience.

Skewed data problem

Suppose you must predict if a random person on the street has the flu. In a population, 0.1% might be affected by the flu in the summer and 0.5% in the winter. If you're building a flu detector model, a solution could be to predict, *not flu*. Depending on the season, that will be between 99.9% and 99.5% accurate. High accuracy, but still not helpful.

Many AI cases have skewed data like this, so we sometimes use other forms of measurement than simple accuracy. If you use the wrong accuracy calculation, the number can seem impressive, while the solution is unusable.

Accuracy

Accuracy in this context is the term for the most natural way to understand a model's prediction correctness. It's a measurement of how often the model provides the correct answer. Suppose the flu model gives the following outcomes:

- TP: true positive: the model guessed flu, and the subject was sick
- FP: false positive: the model guessed flu, but the subject was healthy
- TN: true negative: the model guessed no flu, and the subject was healthy
- FN: false negative: the model guessed no flu, but the subject was sick

To calculate the accuracy, you would divide the correct outcomes (true positive and true negative) by possible outcomes. That calculation would look like this:

accuracy = (TP + TN)/(TP + TN + FP + FN)

Precision

An alternative is *precision*, a measurement of how often the model guesses flu correctly (TP) compared to how often it guesses flu in total (TP + FP). It's conceptually more challenging to comprehend, but the measurement is often practical. It tells you how certain you can be that a positive guess is correct. That's useful when a false positive is costly. You can think about it as the *sniper measurement*. Precision is a suitable measurement if you only want to shoot when you're sure not to miss. The calculation for precision is:

precision = TP/(TP + FP)

Recall

Recall is a measurement that can be used when the priority is to get as many true positives as possible and, getting false positives is not a major issue. You could call this the machine gun measurement. You'd rather shoot one time too many than miss the target. The calculation for recall is:

recall = TP/(TP + FN)

By dividing the true positives (correctly guessed flu cases) by true positives plus false negatives (guessed no flu but was flu), you get a lower score if you miss a flu case. Assuming you'd rather treat one patient too many for flu than not treat a sick patient, this is an excellent measurement to optimise for.

Confusion matrix

An often-used instrument in artificial intelligence is the *confusion matrix*. This table or matrix visualises where the model confuses labels with each other. It's used to spot challenges in a model. Suppose you have a model that can recognise different dog breeds. A confusion matrix shows which breeds are confused with each other by the model, giving you an overview of which labels (breeds), you could aim to improve. There may be mistakes in the labelling, or there's a lack of data on specific labels. You can see an example of a confusion matrix here.

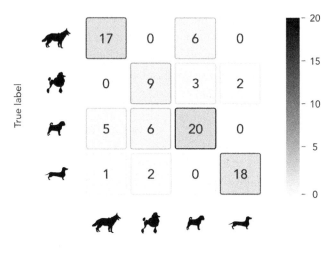

Figure 17: Confusion matrix

One axis represents the true cases (true label). The second axis is what the model has guessed (prediction label) during testing. If you have a good model, the values in the slanted line from the upper left corner to the lower right corner will be as close to 1 as possible.

In the dog breeds recogniser, chances are that Golden Retrievers and Labradors would often be confused by the model despite there being many examples of both, as the two breeds look a lot like each other. In this case, it's easy for humans to predict this result, but it might not be so easy in other cases. The confusion matrix is a useful guide to improving accuracy or where to expect low performance.

Accuracy in generative AI

There's no way to measure accuracy of generative AI. Instead, large generative models are measured through a series of technical measurements indicating their performance. This is not something done by us, who apply AI technology, but those who are building or evaluating the LLM's. They're tested with specific tasks such as NER or through their ability to infer common sense. That's done by trying to answer a riddle or finish a sentence.

For example, in a Hellaswag test a woman is outside with a bucket and a dog. The dog is running around trying to avoid a bath. She...

A. rinses the bucket off with soap and blow dries the dog's head

B. uses a hose to keep it from getting soapy

C. gets the dog wet, then it runs away again

D. gets into a bathtub with the dog

GPT-4, for example, scored a 95% accuracy on this test.

We can't directly know what accuracy our solution has. The model is general purpose, and the use case-specific accuracy might vary greatly. Tools for measuring accuracy are beginning to be developed, but none have really solved the problem yet.

EXPLAINABLE AI

Explainable AI, also called *transparency*, is the ability to explain how a model works and how it turns input data into a prediction. It's used to debug models, understand how performance can be improved, and guide users to better capitalise from the predictions.

Feature importance

One way to explain models is through *feature importance*. Suppose you have a model trying to predict if a customer is about to cancel a subscription. That's commonly known as *churn prediction*.

The model has features such as subscription age and the average time between visits and subscription tier. Feature importance can tell which has the most weight in the model's predictions. It can be used globally, showing how the models weigh the features in general, or locally, describing how the model weighted features for a specific prediction. It could look like this:

Figure 18: Feature importance

Like accuracy, feature measurements can't be read as the truth. When calculating feature importance, different methods can be used, producing results that are not comparable. Using two different methods can provide different results for the same prediction with the same model. Therefore, one should not regard feature importance as a truth but rather as an indication.

For image models, feature importance could look like this:

Figure 19: Image models' feature importance

Explainability in generative AI

So far, explainability in generative AI is simple to explain – there is none. An LLM-based solution won't be able to tell you how it came up with the output it did. For example, if you use ChatGPT to suggest a plan for your next salary negotiation, you will not know what data has affected the result.

If you use an LLM for reasoning and provide access to specific data, then you will get a better sense of explainability. At least it will make user validation faster and the answer easier to understand. For example, you can let an AI agent look through an internal document database of previous support cases to find answers.

Why explainable AI is so hard

Explaining why an AI model comes to a specific prediction is hard, especially when the algorithms are deep learning. The number of parameters and the entangled way the models can come to the prediction might be too much for a human brain to comprehend.

Another reason is that we engineer features when we build models. We might have introduced features that are the results of data manipulation. Knowing that some engineered feature, such as *"running average sales price"*, is integral to a decision doesn't always make sense for users.

When relationships are simple, there's usually no need for AI. It's when relationships become complicated that we use machine learning.

Explaining AI isn't always necessary

The narrative around explainable AI is often that more explainable is better. For a data scientist trying to understand and optimise a model, this might be true. The more they understand the inner workings of a model, the better they can improve it. But that doesn't mean that the model user needs the same understanding. Telling a user that the delivery time was an essential feature when the model decided that a customer wouldn't accept an offer can cause confusion. If the user believes the delivery time isn't crucial in this case, it can undermine trust in the models. It can also lead to users demanding changes to an AI solution that do more harm than good, based on their misunderstood perception of how it works.

It's natural human behaviour to look for patterns and try to understand how things work. Providing information on feature importance that seems simple to the user but is complicated might be more harmful than beneficial. Before making the feature importance available to users, test it with a few of them to learn their reactions.

TESTING RESULTS

Testing your results early with users is helpful to get feedback so you can adjust before spending too much time. But here's the catch. Most people lose confidence in an AI solution that provides incorrect results (in their opinion), even when they're told the AI is in development. That situation must be handled by carefully, choosing suitable and not too many test subjects. As soon as you show even a tiny slice of results to potential users, the story about it will start to manifest. Others will be curious, and the testers will share accuracy percentages and experiences. The impact here will likely lead to either too optimistic or too pessimistic expectations before production.

Every time you run user tests, you run the risk of users losing confidence. If they lose faith in the solution, engaging them further might be hard and hurt adoption.

It's essential to do early tests in a controlled manner. Make sure to do the first testing on a pre-defined test set and do it with the test users. Never send an API or link to a solution for testing without being present. The slightest misinterpretation may negatively affect the users' expectations or experience.

That being said, the value of testing early is high. It can be engaging for the potential users who then will feel included and invested in the project. You will get insight into their reactions, expectations, and what behaviour gave the results. User testing will help you understand if the goals you set with them in the discovery phase are still optimal and how that might affect the decision models.

Imagine you built the forecasting model for SundAI. You're now showing the preliminary results to a test user. Questions like the following could be relevant.

What do you see?

You should show the results without any prior explanation to get an honest first impression. The question reveals that what is obvious to you isn't evident to the user.

How will you act on the predictions?

Ask how they will use the predictions to act. Note if it corresponds to the decision model from the discovery phase. If the answers deviate, investigate why.

How will you test the results?

The test users might have different ways of deciding on the quality of the results. For SundAI, some might compare them with the results of previous forecasting methods, others with actual sales of ice cream, and still others might answer spontaneously.

You may also experience test users picking on the present solution's most challenging cases. That can give insight into what instances the test users expect to be difficult for the AI, such as weekends with events near ice cream stores. It can also reveal that the test user is looking for the most valuable instances to predict.

Much of this should align with what you discovered in the discovery phase, and if there's a discrepancy, it's worth investigating.

Testing generative models

Suppose your business case generates emails for a group of sales reps and you can't measure the accuracy of the output. The business outcomes you're trying to achieve might be faster communication with clients (through writing speed) or more sales (through better emails). These outcomes are hard to measure during development. Writing speed is challenging, as the output must be checked and edited by a sales rep, and testing it requires involving the sales rep.

The result is that domain experts must be closely involved in the development process to help adjust the output and measure the effect on the business outcome you're trying to achieve. The days, when you could rely on data scientist training and fine-tuning alone, until a satisfying solution is ready, are over.

Also, testing with experts versus novices works in an opposite manner in generative compared to predictive AI. Experts get better results when testing generative AI as they can better query (prompt) the models and curate the responses. They also benefit more from generative AI than novices in the field. With predictive AI, it's the opposite.

Skill Level	Predictive AI	Generative AI
Novice	High Benefit	Moderate Benefit
Expert	Moderate Benefit	High Benefit

Table 17: Generative versus predictive AI

You may remember from the first discovery chapter that it could help to ask how a model would benefit a new colleague when interviewing. In generative AI, we should instead test with experts. In predictive AI, experts often agree with the model's output, as the models are trained on their past behaviour and experience. For instance, imagine an AI solution that can detect various plant diseases using image classification. Experts in these diseases don't get much better at correctly recognising diseases, as they already hit the mark very often. Therefore, the gain in predictive AI is that experts become faster, but not better. However, newcomers to a field can get help to be more accurate with predictive AI or even solve tasks they couldn't do before.

Generative AI, on the other hand, is often an accelerator for experts precisely because they know better what questions to ask a Large Language Model and can more easily curate the output. For example, they are better at spotting hallucinations. Beginners in a field cannot do this.

The result is:

If you test a generative AI with experts, expect the value (how much it improves the process) to be lower with average users. If you test generative AI with average users, expect the value to be higher with experts.

The same goes for predictive models:

When testing with experts, expect a higher value when average users get the solution. If you test with average users, expect lower value from expert users.

So, remember to be particular about the skill levels of your test subjects.

MONITORING PHASE: BUILDING AI OPERATIONS

When the AI solution goes into production, the challenges become operational. It's commonly known as *machine learning operations* (MLOps). It covers a wide range of challenges for a live AI solution. The goal is to keep performance on both model accuracy and prediction speed. Sometimes, you'll also want to make updating and adding new models to an AI solution easy. In some settings, you must also comply with regulations and safety constraints. This is the *monitoring phase*.

MONITORING AI ACTIVITIES

- monitoring the model accuracy and drift
- monitoring that the model is live
- performing retraining
- deploying new versions of models

OPERATIONS, FEEDBACK, AND RETRAINING

Feedback and retraining

Retraining in AI refers to the flow of updating a model with the same feature set but with newer or more data. It's done to improve or keep accuracy depending on the drift. In most cases, it is done by feeding the available data to the *training pipeline,* the data cleaning, manipulation, and training with algorithms. In some cases, training is done by only feeding the newly available data and updating the model.

We also often hear retraining referred to as *feedback* or *a feedback mechanism.* I'm not a fan of the names, as it implies feedback on the model output and results, which is rarely the case. For the SundAI forecast model, the retraining would be built using data from actual sales. There's no feedback as such from users or experts explicitly indicating right and wrong guesses.

The retraining pipeline should handle large volumes of training data automatically, with all its different variations. This includes, missing data, different formatting, character sets, or very large amounts. When a data scientist prepares data for models in a development phase, they can manually correct any errors and prepare the data. It requires much more work to build an automatic pipeline than to clean up things found manually.

Drifting and monitoring

Model drift, also known as *drifting* or *model decay,* is when the model and the natural world drift apart. The model and its data are intended to represent the world in which the model should perform well. The result of drifting is less accurate models that translate into less business value. Drifting is sometimes easy to spot by the model showing less and less average certainty. At other times, the model's certainty will remain high while the actual or experienced accuracy falls.

The level of drifting isn't a constant or something you can predict precisely. The best way to defend against too much drift is to monitor it when the AI is live. Most AI solutions will have a gradual natural drift as the world changes. An email classifier will drift as new ways of communicating the same message change. The finance department may have changed the accounting software, and the name is now different when emails refer to it. New clients or products might make this model drift for the support or sales department. In other cases, drift might be a hard change. For example, the COVID-19 pandemic changed practices in only a matter of weeks.

Data drift occurs when the distributions in the data at the time of predictions shift. For example, it could be that the previous churn model is based on gender and age. But if the customer base shifts, from predominantly younger men to older women, we experience data drift. Since models are typically strongest where the data is more dense, such a shift can lead to lower prediction quality.

Concept drift is when there's a fundamental change in the environment. For the churn predictions model, that could be a change of customer preferences. If customers no longer have the same preferences as before, behaviour that previously indicated customers would not cancel their subscription may now mean the opposite. With concept drift, the model or data will not reflect this change. This means that the model's confidence score will still be high, but the actual accuracy will decrease.

Upstream drift is when the data pipeline starts to drift. It could be due to less accurate labelling or data quality. In Paperflow, we saw this happen when we quickly scaled our data labelling operation, as new employees were a relatively more significant part of the team.

Monitoring is often done through a dashboard or alarms sent when the accuracy falls beneath a certain threshold. Sometimes that will call for manual or automated retraining of the model. At other times, it calls for an investigation on what causes the drift.

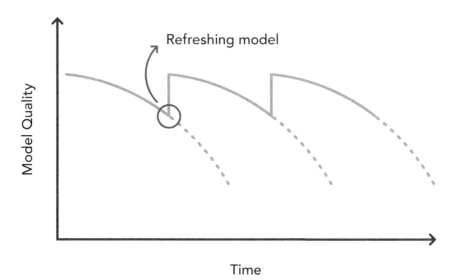

Figure 20: Drifting and monitoring

Some AutoAI solutions, such as Google's Vertex AI, have monitoring and drift measurement available with the click of a button. Others like Neptune and Arize can monitor the model's performance and explain the decline reasons.

AI Governance

AI governance refers to the policies, processes, and practices used to ensure that AI solutions systems are aligned with company compliance and regulations. AI governance has been an increasingly used term in recent years. AI has moved from experimental innovation, often exempt from internal or external regulations to daily operations. As a result, AI governance has become more prevalent. The goal of governance is to mitigate the risks that come with deploying AI.

Managing risks

AI is often called "decision-making at scale". AI solutions can make predictions in milliseconds where humans would spend minutes or hours. Doing things faster is often better for business but it may increase risk. Mistakes will probably magnify the consequences if something goes wrong at a scale thousands of times faster.

Managing risks in AI starts with decision modelling. Choosing the proper decision levels and stating predetermined actions based on predictions makes risks visible. Like many other aspects of AI governance, this must be considered before development starts.

A way to handle governance is to introduce organisation-wide regulations and standards that can be applied to any machine learning and AI solution.

There's one problem, though. The job of writing this compliance is usually given to the legal department. Legal experts rarely have any experience or prior knowledge of AI and can be lost when a governance request lands on their table. Most legal teams settle on the better safe than sorry approach. This makes compliance in some areas too tight and unnecessarily limits AI adoption while simultaneously leaving giant loopholes in other areas. The only cure is knowledge. The more insights into AI the legal team have, the better your chances of having sound regulations.

Governance through culture

Another way to handle governance without having to implement rigorous rules is through culture. This is often more effective than standards and regulations for two reasons:

- You can't do a complete rule-based or oversight-based governance on AI.
- No tools or simple rules can fully limit such invasive technology.

The idea here is to guide through culture and values, let people decide how to use AI, and be responsible for their actions. For example, if a company's culture and norms are customer-centric, no customer support would copy/paste a ChatGPT result without reading it.

Culture is, in my experience, both the most effective and cheapest solution to governing AI.

Ethics

Discussions on AI governance often involves a debate on *ethical* issues. How do we ensure that our application of AI conforms with moral and ethical principles and values? How do we avoid negative consequences of implementing AI, such as the unfair treatment of groups or individuals?

When we apply AI technology for internal purposes, we can use our current ethical standards and values. If we are in full control of the technology and the consequences of using it only impact upon us, then we don't need to make additional ethical considerations.

I must state though, that the approach to ethics in AI given here is the one I see fits best. AI ethics is subject to much debate, and many disagree with this approach and prefer AI specific ethics codes and regulations.

Approving new deployments

Another part of governance is the practical task of deploying new or retrained models into production. You can set up project - or organisation - wide rules on when and on what terms you can deploy models. It's often done with a checklist like this:

- check the confusion matrix
- no deployment unless the accuracy, precision or recall is at least X
- run ten manual predictions from a predetermined dataset
- test for bias with an automated test
- two people check off on the deployment
- never deploy on a Friday (a crime in any IT!)

Some teams also run a shadow production setup (an identical production flow from which users don't see results) for a while before deploying a model.

CHAPTER 11
IMPLEMENTATION PHASE – AI AND HUMANS

The challenges of adopting an AI solution often stem from a lack of understanding of new technology and fear of the unknown, which can be overcome by building confidence in the solution. This confidence is what we aim to achieve in the implementation phase.

During the implementation phase, you aim to ensure that users adopt the solution without resistance and are satisfied with its intended features.

Sometimes, there's a limited number of users, which is usually the case for internal solutions. That usually only needs a short implementation phase. At other times, you adopt external users, meaning a continuous implementation phase for the entire solution lifetime. The latter was the experience we had in Paperflow.

WHAT MAKES IMPLEMENTATION SO IMPORTANT?

Every AI solution needs users; without them the potential value remains unrealised. Take SundAI's sales forecasting, for instance – if nobody adopted this tool, its business impact would be zero. Moreover, competent usage is key. Users must understand how best to act on the solution's output. This involves discerning the reliability of the output and its practical applications. For example, an AI solution writing responses for support emails requires training support staff to review and refine these before customer dispatch. Deciding when to manually check AI outputs and how to efficiently adjust them is a skill that develops over time. Until then, using an AI solution might be less efficient than manual response drafting, especially when users are pressed for time.

It seems logical that user adoption is essential for a solution's value, yet AI solution implementation in organisations is often neglected. Getting users to embrace a solution is harder and more time-consuming than most expect, leading to the underuse or misuse of otherwise valuable AI solutions.

The challenges stem from several factors:

Designers see the full value of their solution. When you've created a solution, its benefits seem obvious, and you expect users to eagerly embrace it. However, this insight and enthusiasm are often absent in new users, who lack your knowledge.

Users perceive the world differently. My experience at Paperflow showed that users with identical tasks had varying perceptions of a solution's value. Winning total adoption from all users becomes increasingly challenging as you approach 100% and strive to persuade the last holdouts.

Users are constantly bombarded with new things. Potential users are usually busy with their own priorities. For instance, SundAI's Store Managers juggle store operations, purchasing, customers, and staff. A new forecasting tool initially seems more disruptive than beneficial, creating a classic catch-22 scenario.

AI solutions can be hard to grasp for users and can induce fear and resistance. Understanding AI outcomes and their reliability can be daunting, often fuelling resistance.

All these challenges, except the last, are common in adopting any solution, not just AI. However, AI solutions face greater resistance due to their complexity and interpretative nature, resulting in fewer potential users willing to invest time in them.

To realise the dream value of your solution, these challenges must be addressed. Otherwise, all the hard work invested becomes futile. This chapter provides tools to tackle these challenges.

STARTING THE IMPLEMENTATION PHASE

The goal of the implementation phase is to achieve user adoption, correct usage, and sustained engagement. This involves several steps:

- Decide how to measure your implementation's success and act on that measurement.
- Identify willing adopters and those hesitating.
- Ensure the solution is effectively 'sold' to potential users.
- Recognize potential resistance and strategize to manage it.
- Build trust among users.

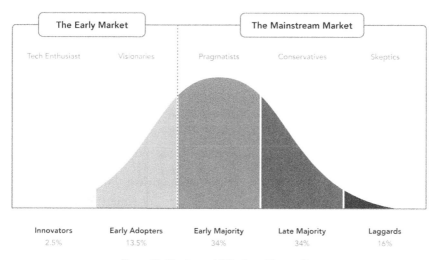

Figure 21. The Law of Diffusion of Innovation

A key piece of advice for starting AI solution implementation is to begin where users are willing and able. In the seminal book on innovation and technology, "Crossing the Chasm," Geoffrey Moore outlines the "technology adoption lifecycle," categorising people based on their readiness to try new technology. Adoption should progress from left to right across this spectrum. For instance, the "Early Majority" won't adopt anything not already successful among "Innovators" and "Early Adopters," as they avoid initial teething problems. On the extreme right are "Laggards," the last to embrace change.

It's noteworthy that everyone has different positions on this curve in various contexts. A colleague's past reluctance doesn't necessarily predict future resistance.

For successful adoption, start with the most enthusiastic individuals. While some prefer a 'big bang' launch or department-by-department rollout, it's often more effective to begin with the most eager employee in each department. Only after they are satisfied with the solution will others consider trying it.

BEFORE THE IMPLEMENTATION PHASE

THE IMPLEMENTATION PHASE REVEALS DISCOVERY FAILURES

Challenges during implementation may arise from decisions made during discovery. Without a secure solution fit for the given challenge, user adoption may be resistant. However, it can be difficult to distinguish whether challenges originate from discovery or implementation, which is crucial because the cure varies significantly.

Implementing new systems can be challenging, with low adoption and resistance common. While the reason for this may sometimes be people's unwillingness to change, often the root cause lies in the discovery phase. The impact of these challenges may not become apparent until implementation, leading to misplaced efforts in training and getting people onboard. That can lead to frustration for management and annoyance for users. Management gets frustrated with the lack of progress, and the users become increasingly annoyed with the added attention they're asked to give to the solution.

If the cause of user resistance is a failure to design a solution that meets their needs and preferences during the discovery phase, adoption may be difficult or impossible. To address this, you need to separate the discovery and implementation-rooted challenges.

Here are the signs that the challenges stem from discovery:

- Users who enthusiastically try out the solution stop using it shortly after. It suggests that the need exists since some users adopted it, but the solution wasn't right, so they quit.
- Users provide feedback on tangible solution features and results. It suggests that they gave it an honest attempt.
- Users disagree if the system works as intended. It suggests that the problem definition and alignment in discovery weren't sufficient.
- The frustration from users is aimed at the solution and not the time and effort they have to put into it.
- Signs of implementation challenges look like this:
- Users aren't even attempting to use the solution. It suggests they have not embraced the idea.
- Users are ready to prove the solution is inaccurate before seeing it, as they don't believe that AI can assist in their complex jobs.
- Feedback is shallow or abstract. Users will make statements such as "The solution will take away our customer relationship" given that the solution automates a sales process. This suggests a fear of a lost sense of control.
- Feedback is hypothetical such as, "What if X happens. How will the system handle that?" where X is a rare case in the process. It suggests that users haven't been explained the role of the new solution in processes.
- The users ask what parameters (features) the model uses to make predictions. That suggests a lack of confidence in the solution that you must build in this phase.

If the challenges are rooted in the discovery phase, the solution is to return to the discovery phase and revisit the activities. That can involve small solutions such as a better user experience or a total rework of the solution. If the challenges are rooted in the implementation, the techniques in this chapter need more effort.

Challenges from both implementation and discovery can be present. If that's the case, discovery is to be visited first.

ACHIEVING ADOPTION

The primary objective of the implementation phase is to achieve adoption. To do so, you need to measure the number of users who adopt the solution and how they use it. It's essential to market and sell the solution internally. You must address the challenge of establishing trust in the solution's accuracy, reliability, and security.

YOU GET WHAT YOU MEASURE

You aim for adoption, so let's measure that. Many forget this when implementing a new AI solution.

A large corporation's business intelligence department once tried to measure service adoption. They were building dashboards for other departments to monitor operations and sales. They suspected that not all dashboards were being used, so they did the obvious. They made a dashboard to track the other dashboards' adoption and use. It turned out that only 20% of the live dashboards were being used. Among that 20%, many were rarely used. All were still being maintained, and licences were paid for the dashboard software but apparently for no reason.

How could that happen?

The reason is that initiating and adopting a new solution are almost two different projects, and there may be little overlap between the people involved. The CFO of SundAI might have seen the need for better forecasting to do better shift planning, while the local store managers are the users who will need to adopt.

Without measuring adoption, you won't be able to determine the success or value of your AI solution. You won't know if your initiatives to engage new users are sufficient or should be increased.

Set goals for adoption

Establishing a goal for how many people should use your AI solution and discussing it openly is essential. This goal can also be used to determine how much effort is required to achieve it. You can plan your strategy and allocate resources by setting a goal for adoption.

In addition, you need to monitor whether users continue to use the AI system. This will help you understand the solution's long-term success and whether any issues must be addressed. Users might start using the solution initially but slip back into old habits after a while.

Measuring whether users use the AI system as intended is also meaningful. Some users may try to find workarounds, or misuse it if they find it challenging or don't understand its intention. By monitoring usage, you can identify any misuse or areas for improvement.

The final critical measure is user satisfaction. Measure it at implementation and continually from then on. It's best to collect satisfaction data anonymously to ensure honest feedback. The *net promoter score* (NPS) is a straightforward measure of satisfaction. It's a simple and effective way to gauge how likely users are to recommend your AI solution to others. That's valuable, even if a recommendation isn't an option. NPS score is a metric ranging from 1 to 10. On a scale of 0 to 10, (1 to 10 or 0 to 10?) users are asked to rate how likely they'd be to recommend the product or service to others. Those who respond with a score of 9 or 10 are considered promoters, while those who respond with 0 to 6 are considered detractors – 7 or 8 is neutral. The NPS is calculated by subtracting the percentage of detractors from the percentage of promoters.

ADOPTION IS A MARKETING TASK

You've built an AI solution for your company and are ready to implement it.

Congratulations on your job as your AI solution's sales and marketing manager! Your task is to create a compelling story that highlights current challenges and the benefits of the new solution. You'll need to identify your target group, book meetings, follow up, and close agreements for users to start.

Many forget that the new solution is a disruptive element that, to the users, means having to learn new procedures, stop the work they're hired to do for a while, and risk making mistakes they don't know how to handle. Therefore, you must sell the solution as if you were selling on the open market. Borrow as much as you can from traditional marketing and sales when you launch a new AI solution in your company.

In addition, remember that even though the AI solution is built internally, it still competes with other existing solutions and tasks. At SundAI, the forecasting solution competes with manual forecasting every day. It's also in competition with not doing forecasting at all. You must ensure that the new solution is preferred and that users adopt it over other options.

HUMANS FIND PATTERNS

Humans are extraordinarily good at finding patterns. In fact, we're a little too good. That's why zodiac signs are a thing. When we implement AI solutions, users seeing patterns in the predictions can make them lose trust or make mistakes.

When AI models fit too close to the training data making, they may show high accuracy in test evaluations but significantly underperform in real-world applications. We call that *overfitting*. When humans do this, it's called *apophenia* or *patternicity*.

Finding patterns is a way to make sense of the world, solve problems and, in the end, survive. This is a valuable trait, but when adopting AI systems that produce predictions we do not comprehend, we may make invalid conclusions, as will be unfolded below. We act on it if we think we've figured out a pattern. If the pattern turns out to be wrong, then we make mistakes.

In Paperflow, the book-keepers were good at finding these patterns. They did it even more when they wanted to be helpful and provide as specific feedback as possible. I even once convinced a book-keeper that the model wasn't relying on colours in the invoice. She was confident that a red colour at the bottom of an invoice would initiate a specific error.

When users perceive non-existent patterns, it can lead to changes in their behaviour. If users anticipate a specific cause and effect, they may modify their actions accordingly. For example, suppose the book-keeper believes that the colour red is causing issues. In that case, she may attempt to eliminate the colour from documents or find a way to bypass the AI system, which could decrease productivity, even though the AI is still in use. These scenarios can be challenging to diagnose and resolve.

Users may also distrust a solution, even if it has no deficiencies, due to perceiving non-existent patterns. They may not communicate the patterns they've observed, making it difficult to clarify that they don't exist.

To address these problems, it can be helpful to explain how the AI solution functions. Additionally, being physically present during the implementation phase can be highly beneficial. It enables you to identify patterns before they gain traction and become accepted as the truth.

GAINING TRUST OR TREATING FEARS AND INSECURITIES

AI adoption is impeded by insecurity and fear among potential users, which must be understood and addressed to lower barriers to adoption.

While many refer to these concerns as a lack of trust in AI solutions, your goal should be to achieve confidence among users that the technology will perform as intended and without unintended consequences. Trust in AI per se is neither a possible nor helpful goal.

The goal is to achieve confidence among users that the AI solution will perform in a way that provides value and doesn't come with unintended or unpredictable side effects. That's difficult due to the nature of the technology.

The best way to instil confidence in users is to let them adopt and experience the benefits of the AI solution first-hand. Until users have experienced the technology's benefits, they may be hesitant to adopt it.

How do you get this adoption? Handle and acknowledge the insecurities you can before adoption and pick the right users to adopt first as explained in the beginning of this chapter.

THE PROBLEM

What is trust anyway?

The definition of trust is that it involves two parties, with one party being willing to be vulnerable and the other doing their best to avoid causing harm or taking advantage of the vulnerable party.

Recognising that no AI solution can guarantee the type of trust described is vital. While AI is designed to generate the most accurate predictions, it doesn't have the will to actively avoid hurting or exploiting anyone. For example, suppose SundAI's sales forecasting solution predicts a significant increase in sales on a particular day. In that case, it may not consider the potential financial loss or embarrassment resulting from a surplus of employees with no customers. Conversely, if the solution predicts lower-than-expected sales, it may not factor in the cost of disappointing customers and the negative impact on the business. In both cases, the AI system will simply generate the best possible prediction based on available data. Even LLMs can't be trusted, despite giving results that appear trustworthy (or not).

Avoid placing your trust in AI – that's counter-productive. If you suggest that users trust an AI solution, you imply that the technology can actively prevent negative consequences. This isn't the case. The role of AI is to provide predictions based on available data. It isn't inherently untrustworthy but rather a tool or machine to be handled with proper care.

Fear and insecurity

Insecurity is a dominant force driving organisational decision-making, including adopting new technology. While the term "fear" may seem intense, it accurately describes the underlying feeling. However, I'll use the word "insecurity" instead.

Adopting innovative solutions and technology can provoke numerous insecurities, particularly in AI. That's due to a variety of factors, including the newness of AI and its conceptual complexity, which makes it challenging to anticipate the consequences of its deployment.

The most common insecurities observed in the context of AI include:

Becoming incompetent at your job. AI is a paradigm-shifting technology, and a new paradigm will make experts of the old paradigm fear that they're no longer the experts.

Fear of the unknown. We're inherently afraid of anything we don't understand. We're wired by nature to restrain from uncertainty as it represents potential threats. When we encounter something unfamiliar, our brains perceive it as a potential danger, triggering a fear response.

Loss of control. We become insecure when we feel responsible for an outcome but can't understand or control the underlying factors.

Fear of costs. Adopting new technology often comes with a price tag in time and money. For most people, losing time is the worst thing they can imagine. Some people will be reluctant to invest in something they're unsure about or don't fully understand.

All these insecurities must be understood and handled while we adopt a new AI solution with users.

SOLUTION

To achieve adoption of AI solutions, you need to:

- provide knowledge to potential adopters
- address the insecurities associated with the new technology
- leverage explainability in AI

Knowledge

General knowledge of AI fosters enthusiasm for the technology. Communicating what it is and how it works can help promote the adoption of AI solutions. Additionally, communicating the specific features of an AI model and the rationale behind the solution's design can reduce insecurity.

It's also possible to explain each individual output through explainable AI. However, explainable AI isn't helpful in every context. (We'll look at that more closely further down).

Law of diffusion in innovation

The Law of Diffusion in Innovation provides a framework for understanding how new technologies are adopted. By identifying different types of adopters and their characteristics, this law can help us understand why some people are more receptive to new technology than others.

Most people don't willingly adopt new solutions. Only 2.5% are innovators who are the first to adopt, and 13.5% are early adopters, making up a total of 15% of all people. That means the remaining 85% are reluctant to adopt new solutions until they've seen them proven successful by others.

This knowledge can help promote the adoption of AI solutions in several ways:

Targeting early adopters: Early adopters make up a significant portion of the population likely to try new technology. Targeting this group can help accelerate the adoption process. This can be done by identifying the early adopters among your potential users. You can tailor your communication towards them before even considering the remaining 85%. This greatly limits your efforts and makes it easier to communicate. When it comes to internal AI solutions, you can allow only early adopters to test them.

Providing social proof: The Law of Diffusion in Innovation suggests that most people are reluctant to adopt new technology until they see others use it successfully. Providing social proof through testimonials, case studies, or endorsements from influential figures can help convince more people to try new technology. You can get that from the early adopters, even those inside an organisation.

Use the decision model in communication.

The decision model outlined in Chapter 8 can help address concerns related to the uncertainties of the unknown and potential costs. By going through each prediction, confidence, and action combination, you can explain:

- scenarios in which actions are automated versus those requiring human intervention
- the particular actions that will be taken and their intended consequences

By engaging in this exercise, you can reduce the unknown factors associated with AI implementation and make the resulting solution more comprehensible and tangible for users in their everyday work.

Recognise the fear

It can be useful to compile a list of potential issues and even a worst-case scenario list when discussing the potential outcomes of an AI solution. Although this may appear to amplify insecurity, individuals are often more accepting of risks when proactively presented with possible negative consequences. This is akin to how therapists encourage those with anxiety to vocalise their fears, as doing so can alleviate some of the apprehension associated with them. Asking, "what is the worst that can happen?" can be a useful tool to help identify and mitigate potential risks related to implementing the AI solution.

For example, let's consider SundAI's current forecasting solution. The potential worst-case scenarios are:

a) The model makes a grossly inaccurate prediction. This results in too much or too little ice cream being purchased and too few or too many staff members showing up for work which causes a financial loss. In this case, the solution can be refined or removed from service altogether.

b) The predictions are so far off that the solution is temporarily taken out of service, requiring everyone to revert to the previous methods. While inconvenient, this is a manageable outcome.

When viewed objectively, neither of these incidents is catastrophic. In fact, they're both fixable, and planning for how to address these scenarios in advance can be beneficial.

It's okay to be insecure

A common mistake when addressing insecurities within an organisation is attempting to convince people to have confidence in a new and improved solution simply because it's novel. For those of us who are excited about innovative new approaches, it can be tempting to dismiss others as resistant to change or "old-school."

This attitude is counterproductive. Dismissing people's concerns or telling them they're wrong for feeling insecure only increases resistance. Instead, listen to and acknowledge individuals' insecurities about new AI solutions, emphasising that feeling apprehensive is normal.

It's worth noting that even AI predictions (which may be highly accurate) aren't infallible. These models are designed with the understanding that they may fail and produce incorrect results.

Explainability *might* increase adoption

The concept of explainable AI can also be employed as a solution. For example, suppose SundAI's forecasting model predicts a surge in customer traffic. In that case, it may be beneficial to display the underlying factors behind the prediction, such as the occurrence of a local event. If you allow users to validate this information, they can gain greater confidence in the accuracy of the prediction. Users often request explainability to understand better how the AI model arrives at its decisions. It helps them feel more at ease with the solution and increases their confidence in its predictions.

Sometimes explainability can be more problematic than helpful. For instance, the explanations are often not as straightforward as attributing the prediction to a single feature. The whole point of AI is that it can recognise and analyse complex patterns, often more intricate than humans can comprehend. Since the forecast is based on interrelated features, explaining the prediction can be as difficult as generating it.

For example, at SundAI, the number of customers can be influenced by both local events and the weather. However, suppose that every time conditions are favourable, a pop-up ice cream shop opens during a local event, resulting in a loss of customers for SundAI. In that case, the forecaster may detect this signal and adjust the predicted number of customers downward. The model doesn't know that the reason for the change is the pop-up ice cream shop. It can only explain that having both good weather and a local event means a slightly lower number of customers than if only one of these factors were present. Many other variables can also be at play, making explainability less explanatory than expected.

You might recognise the feeling as an expert in a field trying to explain why something is a good choice requires you to describe a lot of underlying mechanisms. As a result, you might decide it's better to be brief to avoid confusion or someone jumping to the wrong conclusion. (This is the patternicity mentioned above.)

This phenomenon can also lead to a loss of user confidence, as they may think something is wrong with the model and stop using it. Since the behaviour can't be explained, you end up with reduced user confidence and an increased workload due to having to explain the explainable AI.

SENSE OF CONTROL

Loss of a sense of control is one of the insecurities that can prevent the adoption of an AI solution. Experts often resist changes when they no longer have complete control over the output but still feel responsible for it. When you delegate some of your decision-making or information generation to an AI system, you naturally relinquish some degree of control. This loss of control can be legitimate, or it may simply be a feeling. Regardless, it can be daunting for many people, particularly those who are considered experts in their field.

As you implement AI systems, consider the user's sense of control. Initially, at Paperflow we believed that allowing users to submit documents and receive a response without navigating a frontend system was a significant advantage. However, we soon realised that enabling users to provide feedback to the AI was critical to their satisfaction. In particular, experts in their field often need to provide feedback and use their expertise to feel fulfilled in their work. Active feedback can help these individuals regain a sense of control over the AI system.

Having a "feedback button," even if it does nothing, can make a difference to the user. In fact, this solution has helped address a specific problem in many cities worldwide. As a pedestrian waiting at a traffic light, it can often feel like you've been waiting forever. This feeling can increase the likelihood of jaywalking. To counter this, many cities have installed buttons at traffic lights that pedestrians can press to indicate their intention to cross. However, in many of these cases, the button serves little more than a placebo function, simply providing the user with a sense of control. Nonetheless, this simple addition can effectively reduce the incidence of jaywalking and increase safety.

THE KASPAROV PERSPECTIVE ON AI ADOPTION

There are several potential challenges with adopting AI solutions, which might make it seem daunting. However, it's doable to overcome, and I would like to add some perspective from Garry Kasparov, the renowned world chess champion. He provides valuable insight in his Ted Talk, "Don't Fear Intelligent Machines. Work With Them."[1] Despite his extensive chess knowledge, Kasparov felt uneasy when IBM's Deep Blue chess machine finally defeated him. His doubts and fears were human, and he wondered if his beloved game was over. However, Kasparov later discovered that doomsayers were wrong. Chess continued to thrive even with the advent of machines.

Kasparov's conclusion was that a weak human chess player supported by a machine is superior to a machine alone. Furthermore, this combination was even more effective than a strong human player, a machine, and an inferior process. This was demonstrated when a group of amateur chess players triumphed over supercomputers and chess grandmasters.

Despite being the ultimate expert in his field, Kasparov experienced the same feelings and doubts as any expert adopting AI solutions. Nevertheless, he saw the advantage and the purpose and encouraged others to guide their users to the same destination.

Hopefully, this example demonstrates that converting your users into AI enthusiasts is possible over time.

SOCIAL CONTRACT

When we work with others, we often operate under social contracts, which are cultural agreements on how to behave. However, when we implement AI, these social contracts may be terminated, leading to changed behaviour. Dan Ariely's book *Predictably Irrational* explains this concept and explores how humans behave irrationally in structured and predictable ways.[2] While the book isn't directly about AI, it provides valuable insight into understanding what happens when machines replace humans.

Ariely emphasises the power of social contracts between people and their impact on behaviour. This applies to understanding the effects of implementing AI, which can disrupt social contracts and change how people behave. It's essential to consider these dynamics when designing and deploying AI solutions. By understanding how social contracts shape behaviour, we can better anticipate the impacts of AI and work to mitigate any negative effects.

Ariely describes a kindergarten in Israel which faced an issue with parents picking up their children late, resulting in day-care workers having to stay beyond their working hours. To tackle this problem, they introduced a monetary fine for late pickups. However, the outcome was unexpected. After the introduction of the fines, parents started picking up their children even later.

Ariely's theory suggests that the social contract between humans is stronger than the transactional. In this case, the day-care worker who appeals to the social contract by saying, "Pick up your children on time so I can get home to my own children," creates a significantly higher cost than "If you pick up your children late, you have to pay a fee." The fine is now merely a transaction; parents might see it as a way to buy extra time. It could be perceived as a good deal, thus undermining the initial intention of the fine.

This example highlights the significance of social contracts in human behaviour. However, this social contract is absent when adopting AI, and a new dynamic must be considered. Replacing humans with AI can remove the social contract from the equation, resulting in a change in user behaviour. For example, if a robot replaces a human in cleaning a workspace, it's unlikely that people will treat the area with the same respect as before. This may not be an issue regarding the amount of cleaning required, but if the AI is trained based on current human behaviour or business cases, it might not achieve the expected results.

People often know they're interacting with AI in text messages (like ChatGPT) when it communicates on behalf of a company. Think about the full sales AI that was described earlier. Will people lie or try to cheat the AI than they would a human? Maybe they'll try to get a discount by saying they were promised it or that something bad happened that they need compensating for.

Ariely's theory says yes. You could try it a few times to see if it's possible. (Remember that it's a requirement to disclose to users that they're talking to AI under the new EU AI Act.)

So, when deploying AI, be prepared to change people's processes and habits. Monitoring behaviour will help you ensure it doesn't change in unexpected ways. For example, it could negatively impact results if SundAI's sales managers report worse sales data, or they report sales data later due to the automated forecasting process with no human involvement. Additionally, if an AI is trained on data about user behaviour, but they change their behaviour when it is introduced, it may experience a significant deviation from expected results. For example, if a supervisor at a plant previously called out people without safety equipment, but now an AI in a camera in the corner sets off an alarm, employees may hold their hard hats over their heads for the few seconds they pass the camera.

To avoid such disruptions, you must identify where social contracts may be broken when implementing an AI solution. This involves closely examining current processes and the interactions between employees and other stakeholders so you can identify any unwritten agreements that might be impacted. Once these social contracts are identified, you must evaluate whether the AI solution can replace or support these social contracts or if adjustments need to be made to the solution.

SUMMARY

Challenges during the implementation phase may hinder user adoption and impact success. Techniques to overcome challenges include involving end-users in the design process, providing training, and adopting change management strategies. The implementation phase can be internal or external, each with unique considerations. You need effective communication and to build trust with customers for external implementation. AI adoption can be hindered by factors such as explainability, loss of control, and social contracts. To promote adoption, organisations must provide knowledge of AI and its features, address insecurities through communication, and leverage explainability in AI. Only a small percentage of people are innovators and early adopters, so targeting the right users is crucial. Despite challenges, converting users into AI enthusiasts over time is possible. Organisations must focus on addressing challenges during implementation, effectively communicating, and building trust to achieve successful adoption and realise the benefits of AI solutions.

AFTERWORD

In the three years I've been writing this book (and my eight years in AI), AI has changed from a niche technology to a powerful tool every business wants and needs to figure out and handle. It's no longer simply a field for research but an applied technology where what used to involve hard work and loads of code can now be done in minutes. During the last year or so the expansion of generative AI has also changed the playing field dramatically. Still, the approach that works the best for applying the technology and building solutions is no different. The same goes for the tools and techniques for understanding and aligning a problem space with business needs.

Teaching people what AI can do and what it is and giving them a common language and best practice matters even more now that the technology is unavoidable.

I've had the luxury of cherry-picking from best practices that originated as far back as the 1960s, and I find that the user-focused mindset is the one that works. AI is nothing without its users. It doesn't matter what kind of AI or how advanced a solution you build, the same basic human dynamics must be accounted for and handled.

That's why learning the discipline of applying AI and using this method is a long-term strategy. Many people spend a lot of time choosing the right data platform, LLM or cloud provider to give them a strategic advantage. But when you truly understand the discipline, the technology parts will fall into place. Practice will – of course – be your most valuable teacher.

My method is more elaborate in the discovery phase than many other AI methods. That is especially valuable when applying Generative AI, for which there will be many more use cases in the future. Compared to Predictive AI, Generative AI takes away much of the code, retraining flows and prediction pipelines. At the same time Generative AI also comes with infinite output space and much greater complexity. This means that the business understanding, and the softer skills and techniques, often found with the humanist, are becoming ever more important and demand a shift of effort away from technology and towards AI users.

The demand and use of data in AI has also changed. We used to need a lot of structured data to be able to complete AI projects. Generative AI can use our unstructured data and companies can now unlock value that previously seemed unattainable.

Sceptics might say that AI still isn't useful due to its limitations and the fact that it can make "stupid" mistakes. But it's not either/or. There's a time and place for AI; the bottleneck isn't the technology itself but our ability to utilise it. That situation won't change for many years ahead as advances in technology greatly outperform the speed of which societal and business structures can change. This is also where we will see the largest clashes and conflicts. For example, work on the first EU regulation on AI that was agreed upon in December 2023 started in 2015 – during the same eight years I've seen the technology go from niche to powerful and invasive.

Much of the text, reasoning and motivation behind the legislation hasn't changed. It's likely that the gap between technology and the political system will continue to increase. For example, women have had equal rights in the labour market for decades in the Western world, but the number of female CEOs in Denmark (a progressive country in most ways) is still much lower than male CEOs. In fact, more CEOs are named "Lars" than there are female CEOs.

People are conservative when it comes to changing business structures, but technological advances have the opposite trend.

Going forward, the next big thing will be the rise of AI agents – big LLMs that can access the internet, emails, and other documents will be let loose. Chances are it will be like the wild west for a few years, but it will also be extremely productive and valuable.

We're only beginning to learn how to use AI agents. At the time of writing, my company is working on several projects that include agents with access to both the internet and company documents. The biggest issue is that considering the vast opportunities this provides is almost paralysing.

Before long, we will see sophisticated AI models similar to Large Language Models (LLMs) that are multimodal. These models will be capable of processing and generating various types of data, including text, audio, images, and video. This development process is already underway. The output can also be in different data types depending on what the model decides is better. We'll also see a new kind of model for reasoning that in contrast to LLM doesn't use text as the basis.

But remember that AI has no motivations or feelings, so it won't take over the world as some fear!

You might wonder if you should bother building AI solutions now it is being built into all kinds of software. It will soon be in Word, Excel, your browser, whatever you use daily at work and elsewhere. But the field will keep changing. It's similar to the situation with website development. It used to take an experienced developer to code websites, but now you can build your own with Wix, Squarespace or similar. However, there's still a need for web developers, even a lack of them. The same move towards less need for expertise will happen in the AI space. Everyone will be able to make simple AI solutions with a few clicks but the demand for more complex solutions will grow even faster.

Some businesses feel threatened by AI. They've been scrambling to hold on to their market as AI can substitute their services. I've seen cases where clients told a company supplying a service that they'd soon no longer need their solution as AI would be able to do what their product does. The clients failed to consider that software products come with specialised user interfaces that still hold a large part of the value. Such companies have started building AI into their products and will likely be fine.

I am convinced that AI will change the world for the better. Yes, it comes with some ethical problems and inconveniences that will be hard to deal with. Deep fakes and clever LLMs in the hands of criminals can scam people on a huge scale. This will take some effort to fix.

But when we look at the big picture, AI has huge advantages. It will help us diagnose and cure diseases faster, find new vaccines, and eliminate tedious and boring work. It will also mean a huge increase in wealth for everyone – not just the rich. Usually, Western economies grow at 2-3% a year, but recently a study found that AI will most likely make all sectors improve productivity to 7% a year, making it more likely to be the new normal for economic growth.[1]

AI isn't about killer robots going on a killing spree. It isn't about computers conspiring to take over the world. It's about using the intelligence and information we already have in a better, more efficient, more productive, and more beneficial way. It will help us learn more easily, have easier and more equitable access to information, and be more productive.

Change is always worrying, and some people fear the changes AI is bringing. This is often based on misunderstanding what AI actually is and what it can do. We are always in control of AI, and with it we can build a better world.

ACKNOWLEDGMENTS

I want to extend my heartfelt appreciation to everyone who contributed to the creation of this book.

Firstly, I am deeply grateful to Hans Peter Bech for his invaluable role as the editor, providing guidance and expertise throughout the editorial process.

Special thanks to Kim Farnell for her diligent efforts in ensuring the content adheres to British English standards, enhancing the readability and accessibility of the text for all our readers. Jelena Galkina's talent in designing the captivating cover art has indeed brought the book's essence to life, captivating readers from the moment they lay eyes on it. Koen Campman's skilful illustrations have enriched the pages of this book, adding depth and visual appeal to the content within. Emma Crabtree's meticulous proofreading has been instrumental in ensuring the accuracy and clarity of the text and contributed to a polished final product.

I also extend my gratitude to my colleagues at Todai for their unwavering support, dedication, and willingness to engage in experimentation, challenges, and testing. Your input and feedback have been invaluable in refining the methods presented in this book, leading to significant improvements and advancements in our field.

This book stands as a testament to the collaborative efforts of a talented team, and I am genuinely grateful for the contributions of each and every individual involved.

Thank you all for your passion, expertise, and commitment to excellence.

ABOUT THE AUTHOR

In 2015, I co-founded Paperflow, a SaaS company with an AI-based product. I worked there as a product manager and later as CEO. I now run Todai, an AI consultancy in Copenhagen. We have delivered AI solutions to some of Denmark's largest companies and trained hundreds of individuals in the technology.

Over the years, I have taken on numerous roles, including marketing manager and developer. And I have made every conceivable mistake and detour possible in AI. This has given me a comprehensive understanding of AI's technical and business aspects. It has also helped me identify common problems and develop effective ways to address them.

Over the last few years, I learned much about how to – and how not to – work with it. Now more and more people are beginning to work with AI for the first time, I want to share what I know. Hopefully, it will make your AI experience less painful.

———

I run my company AI consultancy Todai in Copenhagen. We build AI solutions, offer advice and teach. If you'd like to get in touch, contact me at dan.rose@todai.ai - https://todai.ai/ .

INDEX

NOTES

2. DEFINING AND DEMYSTIFYING AI

1. T. Mitchell, *Machine Learning* (McGraw Hill, 1997), p. 2.

4. PREPARING YOUR ORGANISATION FOR REAPING THE BENEFITS OF AI

1. "Ny analyse: Danske virksomheder er europamestre i kunstig intelligens," ("New analysis: Danish companies are European champions in artificial intelligence") *SMVdanmark,* 22 February 2022, https://via.ritzau.dk/pressemeddelelse/ny-analyse-danske-virksomheder-er-europamestre-i-kunstig-intelligens?publisherId=13559667&releaseId=13642887 [accessed 21 May 2023].
2. Søren Kierkegaard, *Synspunktet for min forfattervirksomhed* (*The Point of View of My Work as an Author*), (C. A. Reitzel, 1859).

6. INSPIRATION PHASE

1. A pretotype is a concept related to product development and innovation. It refers to creating a simple, low-cost, and often non-functional version of a product idea to quickly test its viability and gather feedback from potential users or customers. The goal of a pretotype is to validate the fundamental concept behind a product before investing significant time and resources in building a fully functional prototype or a complete product.

7. DISCOVERY – UNDERSTANDING THE PROBLEM

1. Daniel Kahneman *Thinking, Fast and Slow* (London: Allen Lane an imprint of Penguin Books, 2011), p. 13.
2. Teresa Torres, *Continuous Discovery Habits* (Oregon: Product Talk, 2021), p. 74.

8. DISCOVERY – DECISION MAKING AND ACCURACY

1. For example, see A. Pluchino, A. E. Biondo and A. Rapisarda, "Talent vs. Luck: the role of randomness in success and failure," *Advances in Complex Systems,* vol. 21, nos

3 and 4 (2018), https://www.worldscientific.-com/doi/pdf/10.1142/S0219525918500145 [accessed 22 May 2023].

9. DATA HANDLING

1. Dan Ariely, *Predictably Irrational: The Hidden Forces That Shape Our Decisions* (London: Harper, 2009), p. 26.
2. Abraham Wald, Centre for Naval Analyses Alexandria VA Operations Evaluation Group, "A Reprint of 'A Method of Estimating Plane Vulnerability Based on Damage of Survivors," (a series of eight memoranda originally published by the Statistical Research Group at Columbia University for the National Defense Research Committee in 1943), 1 July 1980, https://apps.dtic.mil/docs/citations/ADA091073 [accessed 22 May 2023].
3. Nassim Nicholas Taleb, *Fooled by Randomness* (London: Penguin, 2007), p. 4.
4. https://blogs.gartner.com/andrew_white/2021/07/24/by-2024-60-of-the-data-used-for-the-development-of-ai-and-analytics-projects-will-be-synthetically-generated/

10. DEVELOPING AI

1. D. Sculley, Gary Holt, Daniel Golovin, Eugene Davydov, Todd Phillips, Dietmar Ebner, Vinay Chaudhary, Michael Young, Jean-François Crespo and Dan Dennison,"Hidden Technical Debt in Machine Learning Systems," Part of Advances in Neural Information Processing Systems 28 (NIPS 2015), *NeurIPS Proceedings,* https://papers.nips.cc/paper_files/paper/2015/hash/86df7dcfd896f-caf2674f757a2463eba-Abstract.html [accessed 22 May 2023].

11. IMPLEMENTATION PHASE – AI AND HUMANS

1. Garry Kasparov, "Don't fear intelligent machines. Work with them," https://www.t-ed.com/talks/garry_kasparov_don_t_fear_intelligent_machines_work_with_them?language=en [accessed 22 May 2023].
2. Ariely, *Predictably Irrational: The Hidden Forces That Shape Our Decisions.*

AFTERWORD

1. Jan Hatzius, Joseph Briggs, Devesh Kodnani, and Giovanni Pierdeminico, "The Potentially Large Effects of Artificial Intelligence on Economic Growth (Briggs/Kodnni), *Goldman Sachs,* 26 March 2023, https://www.ansa.it/documents/1680080409454_ert.pdf [accessed 22 October 2023].

Printed in Great Britain
by Amazon

41619457R00158